Point of Order

Point of Order

A Profile of Senator Joe McCarthy

by Robert P. Ingalls

G. P. Putnam's Sons, New York

First Impression
Design by Carolyn Craven
Library of Congress Cataloging in Publication Data
Ingalls, Robert P.,
    Point of order.
    Bibliography: p.
    Includes index.
    Summary: Presents a biography of the unknown
first-term senator from Wisconsin who became
world famous in the "nightmare" decade after
World War II by charging that Communists had
infiltrated the government
    1. McCarthy, Joseph, 1908–1957—Juvenile
literature.   2. Anti-communist movements—United
States—History—Juvenile literature.   3. Legislators
—United States—Biography—Juvenile literature.
4. United States. Congress. Senate—Biography—
Juvenile literature. [1. McCarthy, Joseph, 1908–
1957.   2. Legislators]   I. Title.
E748.M143I53   973.918'092'4   [B]   81-10639
ISBN 0-399-20827-5   AACR2

Contents

Acknowledgments

In writing this book I have accumulated a number of debts that I gratefully acknowledge. First and foremost, I relied heavily on the published work of historians and journalists who are listed in the bibliography. The books by Richard M. Fried and Robert Griffith were particularly helpful because they are models of thoroughly researched and perceptively argued studies. In addition, I would like to express my profound appreciation to Richard Fried for his kindness in taking the time to read this manuscript and share his insights. His command of the subject helped improve the text in countless ways, including the elimination of many errors of fact. My editor, Margaret Frith, also deserves credit for her friendly and incisive advice. Of course, I alone am responsible for any errors that remain.

My colleagues at the University of South Florida, especially Steve Lawson and Lou Pérez, continue to provide the encouragement and moral support that make books like this possible.

Finally, I would like to thank members of my family, especially Joèle, Michèle and Marc, who give meaning to everything I do. My parents, to whom this book is dedicated, are the ones who unselfishly gave me the opportunity to study history. For this, and so many other things, I will always be grateful.

For My Mother and Father

Point of Order

1 | "Point of Order"

During the spring of 1954, millions of Americans sat glued to their television sets watching a special daytime program. With an audience estimated at over twenty million people, the enormously popular show actually disrupted the daily life of the country. Many stores reported a noticeable decline in business during the hours it was on the air. On the West Coast, where the show went on the air before 8 A.M. due to the time change, some employers complained that it made people late for work.

The object of this unusual attention was neither a soap opera nor a sporting event, although it had elements of both. The spectacle that gripped the country for over two months was the Army–McCarthy hearings. Televised live from the Capitol in Washington, D.C., this drama pitted the U.S. Army against Joseph R. McCarthy, the junior Senator from Wisconsin. The Army had publicly accused Senator McCarthy of improperly seeking special favors for Private G. David Schine, one of the Senator's staff members who had been drafted. McCarthy in turn claimed that the Army had held Schine "hostage" in order to force the Senator to end an investigation of the Army. This barrage of charges and countercharges led to a U.S. Senate inquiry which became known as the Army–McCarthy hearings.

Running for thirty-six days in the spring of 1954, the televised hearings captured a huge audience. The live telecasts cost the TV networks millions of dollars in lost advertising for canceled shows, but when NBC announced after several days that it would drop complete coverage of the hearings, public protests forced the company to reverse its decision. Americans showed a clear preference for the Army–McCarthy hearings over the usual daytime television programming.

The Senate investigation created a real-life drama of its own. Although not a trial, the hearings often had the flavor of a courtroom battle. Unfriendly witnesses were harshly cross-examined under the glare of TV lights. Lawyers fought over disputed evidence such as fake FBI letters. The television audience could think of itself as a jury trying to get at the truth. The viewers were also placed in the position of eavesdroppers as the open microphones caught senators attacking one another, occasionally in vicious terms. The hearings often erupted into shouting matches that surpassed the fury of family fights on soap operas. Those viewers who were sports fans could pick sides and watch the balance shift between Senator McCarthy and the Army. In fact, many sessions could be summarized by answering the simple question "Who won today's round?"

The hearings were complicated by a large cast of characters, but one figure—Joe McCarthy—stood out above all others. Even before the televised hearings began, McCarthy had made his name well known through his ability to dominate the news. Indeed, it was his presence that guaranteed such a large audience for the Army–McCarthy hearings. A large barrel-chested man with thinning hair, the Senator from Wisconsin had long championed a no-holds-barred approach to politics. (He bragged that someone named "Indian Charlie" had once taught him to hit below the belt when fighting an important battle.)

Although not acting as chairman of the committee that conducted the Army–McCarthy investigation, Senator McCarthy forced himself into the spotlight. His favorite technique was to interrupt the proceedings by demanding, "A point of order, Mr. Chairman, a point of order." (In parliamentary rules, a point of order is raised to point out a violation of correct procedures, and as such it takes precedence over all other motions.) Having gained the floor (and the TV camera), McCarthy would then deliver a speech that frequently created disorder. In this way, he came to dominate the hearings, and he made the phrase "point of order" famous because millions of TV viewers knew it was the cue for the fireworks that often followed.

Five years earlier, few people outside Wisconsin had ever heard of Joe McCarthy. The story of how an unknown first-term senator became world famous is rooted in a period of American history that has been called "the nightmare decade" because "the politics of fear" swept the country. A product of these troubled times, Joe McCarthy is often remembered as the villain who somehow caused all the hysteria. However, much larger forces, beyond the control of any single individual, helped bring about this troubled period. A close look at the crucial decade after World War II will show how the Wisconsin Senator rose to prominence, only to disappear from view after four years of riding high.

2 | "Tail Gunner Joe"

Joe McCarthy was a controversial political figure who lived much of his life in the public eye. Yet no one has published a full-scale biography of McCarthy. Part of the problem is that basic facts and incidents in his life are in dispute. McCarthy himself helped sow the seeds of confusion by giving differing versions of significant events in his life. Although he died in 1957, his private papers have never been opened to historians. Thus books about him, frequently written by authors with very strong feelings for or against him, have occasionally relied on half-truths or rumors to make their case. Nevertheless, most studies agree on the central facts, as well as on McCarthy's basic character traits.

McCarthy's carelessness with the truth confused even the date of his birth. He sometimes gave his birth date as November 9, 1909, sometimes as November 14. Official records place his birth on November 14, but in a different year—1908.

Joseph Raymond McCarthy was the middle child in an Irish Catholic family of nine children. Joe's father, Timothy, was born in this country, but his mother, Bridget, was an immigrant from Ireland. The McCarthy family farmed 142 acres in Grand Chute township of Outagamie County in northern Wisconsin. Like their neighbors, the McCarthys worked hard just to eke out a living from the worn-out soil. Joe was remembered as a hardworking, average boy.

He attended nearby Underhill Country School, a one-room schoolhouse, for all eight primary grades. After graduating from Underhill at the age of fourteen, young McCarthy became a chicken farmer, using land he rented from his father. With money he had saved from odd jobs, the young businessman started with a small flock, and within two years he had some ten thousand chickens, which he sold in Chicago. However, the bottom fell out of his thriving business when he got sick with pneumonia and could not tend to the chickens. Facing ruin at the age of nineteen, Joe gave up farming altogether.

McCarthy packed his bags and moved to the nearby town of Manawa where he became manager of a grocery store. But after several months at this dead-end job he decided he needed to get more education. So, at the age of twenty, Joe started high school in Manawa. With help from the principal, who tutored him, McCarthy finished all four years of work in a single year.

He then set off for Marquette University, a Catholic school in Milwaukee, where he financed his education with odd jobs. He also spent time on extracurricular activities, especially debating and boxing, both of which sharpened his ability as a fighter. Moreover, he got involved in campus politics and won the election for president of his freshman law class. McCarthy showed less interest in his studies. He had started out in engineering, but a poor background in mathematics hampered him. After two years at Marquette, he switched to law, but a job and other outside activities still kept him from devoting full time to his studies. Like many students, he crammed for exams at the last minute and managed to pass; he was helped by his determination and a remarkable memory.

After graduating from law school in 1935, McCarthy was admitted to the Wisconsin bar and he hung out his law shingle in Waupaca, a small city near his birthplace. It was the middle of the Great Depression, and McCarthy had trouble making ends meet. After only eight months on his own, he accepted an offer to join the practice of Michael Eberlein, a successful lawyer in the nearby city of Shawano.

From the start, McCarthy showed more interest in local politics than in the legal world. A Democrat by birth and inclination, he soon headed the area's Young Democratic Club. In 1936 he made his first bid for public office when he ran for district attorney of Shawano County. As a little-known newcomer, he finished third and returned to the obscure life of a country lawyer.

In 1939, McCarthy tried again. He announced his candidacy for the nonpartisan post of judge for Wisconsin's Tenth Circuit, which included the counties of Shawano and his native Outagamie. Few people thought McCarthy had a chance, since he was running against Judge Edgar V. Werner, who had twenty-four years' experience in the post. However, in his uphill fight McCarthy resorted to a highly questionable tactic. He turned the sixty-six-year-old judge into "my 73-year-old opponent," and he implied that Judge Werner was too old to serve another term. McCarthy not only added seven years to the judge's age, he also dropped a year off his own to make himself appear the youngest candidate ever to run for the post. Campaigning under the slogan "Justice Is Truth in Action," McCarthy blitzed the district with speeches, postcards and personal visits with the voters. The result was an upset victory for young Joe McCarthy.

His tactics did not go unchallenged. The supporters of Judge Werner filed a petition charging that McCarthy had violated the state's corrupt-practices law by misrepresenting his opponent's age and spending more campaign funds than permitted. The petition was turned down by the governor, however—a fact that must have encouraged McCarthy, for the methods he had used were the first of many irregularities that arose in his political career.

As a circuit-court judge, McCarthy worked at a furious pace. In clearing up a backlog of about 250 cases, Judge McCarthy sometimes kept his court in session past midnight. He also cut corners by trying cases in record time. McCarthy could produce quick decisions, but justice was not always served. In one famous case, he refused to enforce a law on the grounds that the law was due to expire in six months. When an attorney for the state appealed this decision, Wisconsin's Supreme Court asked for the trial records. Judge McCarthy responded that he had ordered part of the court transcript destroyed because it was immaterial. The Wisconsin Supreme Court denounced McCarthy for "an abuse of judicial power" in not following the law and for his "highly improper" conduct in destroying official records. The court took no other action against him, but the incident showed McCarthy's disregard for the laws he was sworn to uphold.

During World War II McCarthy again showed his willingness to stretch the truth for political purposes. Although he could have avoided military service because judges were exempt, he volunteered for the Marine Corps and received a commission as a first lieutenant. However, he later circulated the story that he had enlisted as buck private and had worked his way up to the rank of officer. This was only the first of many myths he created about his war record in the Pacific, myths he used to get an extraordinary amount of publicity in Wisconsin newspapers.

Like most soldiers, McCarthy served behind the lines, but, unlike others, he later tried to pass himself off as a combat veteran. He did fly on several combat missions, but only as an observer who went along for the ride, sitting in the tail gunner's seat of a dive bomber. Friendly news reporters filed distorted stories about Joe's being a "veteran of a dozen raids" against Japanese positions. Wisconsin newspapers printed the stories along with pictures that showed McCarthy sitting in a dive bomber. Another story reported that Joe had been wounded in action. Actually he had injured his foot when he fell down during a celebration aboard ship. On the basis of these exaggerated stories, McCarthy later referred to himself as "Tail Gunner Joe." In fact most of his war work was done at a desk, where he served as an intelligence officer evaluating the missions of Marine bomber pilots.

While he was still in the Marine Corps, Captain McCarthy ran in the Republican primary for the U.S. Senate. In July 1944 he got thirty days' leave, which he used to return home and campaign against Republican Senator Alexander Wiley. A former Democrat, McCarthy never explained his switch to the GOP (Grand Old Party), except to say, "It was an advantage to be a Republican with a Democratic name." He might have added that Wisconsin was a strong Republican state and that a Democratic candidate had little chance to get elected.

Running for office raised other questions, some of which once again involved possible violations of the law. Wisconsin's state constitution barred judges from holding another public office during the term for which they were elected, and McCarthy's term as a judge was not over. Captain McCarthy also disregarded military rules that prohibited a soldier from taking political positions. Crisscrossing the state in full uniform, he opened campaign speeches with disclaimers such as "If I were able to speak, I would say . . ."

McCarthy lost to Alexander Wiley in the 1944 primary, but his reputation as "Tail Gunner Joe" was firmly fixed in the voters' minds.

In February 1945, six months before the end of the war against Japan, Captain McCarthy resigned his commission and returned to Wisconsin, where he once again became Judge McCarthy. Still thinking about higher office, he began speaking to groups around the state about his war experiences, many of which were pure fiction. But his image as the limping Marine hero grew.

McCarthy still had his eyes set on the U.S. Senate. In 1946, Senator Robert M. La Follette, Jr., was up for reelection. A twenty-year veteran of the Senate, La Follette had considerable advantages, not the least of which was the most famous name in the state. His father had served as governor and U.S. senator, and his brother had also held the governor's seat. However, "Young Bob" La Follette had been elected most recently on the ticket of the Progressive Party, a third party created in Wisconsin during the 1930s. Originally a Republican, La Follette disbanded the Progressive Party and returned to the GOP in 1946. This gave McCarthy his opening, since many conservative Republicans resented La Follette as a liberal renegade. Furthermore, La Follette's liberal supporters, especially working people, would probably not follow him into the Republican Party.

While Senator La Follette remained on the job in

Washington, Judge McCarthy took the state by storm. Traveling from town to town, he campaigned as "Tail Gunner Joe," the war hero who would clean up the mess in Washington. His slogan became "Congress Needs a Tail Gunner." McCarthy also attacked La Follette with the farfetched charge that he was a "war profiteer." On one occasion, he accused the Senator of "playing into the hands of the Communists by opposing world co-operation." Running against a politically weakened man, McCarthy won a slim primary victory by five thousand votes.

In the general election, McCarthy had other advantages that helped Republicans across the country. With the world finally at peace, Americans were increasingly dis-satisfied with shortages that kept prices high. The GOP slogan, "Had Enough?," asked Americans to vote against the Democrats who had controlled Congress since 1932. Like other Republican candidates, McCarthy benefited from the nation's mood, and he won Wisconsin's Senate race by an overwhelming margin.

McCarthy's victory was clouded by his violation once again of the state's constitutional ban on a judge's running for a second public office. McCarthy dismissed the legal question as "a small matter, entirely technical." How-ever, several years later a Wisconsin lawyer called for disbarment of McCarthy. In 1949, the state board of bar commissioners recommended this step, but the Wisconsin Supreme Court refused. The high court admitted that McCarthy had run for office "in violation of the terms of the constitution and laws of Wisconsin," but it ruled that the act was unlikely to be repeated and that the voters, after all, had elected McCarthy.

Joe McCarthy's performance in the Senate did not im-prove his reputation. The thirty-eight-year-old newcomer proved to be a maverick, not so much in his votes as in his total disregard of Senate rules and customs. In speeches on the Senate floor, he attacked colleagues personally— Democrats and Republicans alike. Moreover, he distorted facts, and even lied, in order to make a point.

As a U.S. senator, McCarthy flaunted his vulgarity. He frequently invited newspapermen to photograph him unshaven and in his shirtsleeves with a drink at hand. When he put on a suit, it usually looked as if he had slept in it, which in fact was sometimes the case. A man of great energy, he could spend a day in the Senate, work that evening in his office, pass much of the night drinking and playing poker, and then catch a few hours' sleep on the couch in his office.

In addition to his hunger for publicity, McCarthy seemed to want to be liked, even by those he hit below the belt. Outgoing and friendly, McCarthy seemed incapable of genuine hate. After viciously attacking someone in a public hearing, he could meet the same person in a Senate corridor and give him a hug and a smile. He insisted that everyone call him "Joe," and he even listed himself that way in official records.

For McCarthy the world was a stage, and he simply played a role. Like any other actor he repeated his lines with great feeling, but he did not necessarily believe them. He showed that he could change positions, even political parties, as easily as an actor changes costumes.

During the first three years of his Senate term, McCarthy won a reputation as the faithful servant of several lobbyists. These were the paid representatives of special-interest groups, such as corporations, and they could be found in the lobbies of Congress trying to persuade lawmakers to vote a certain way. In legislative battles, the junior Senator from Wisconsin seemed less concerned with principles than with the impact of bills on his new friends among lobbyists.

McCarthy's first Senate battle won him the nickname of "Pepsi-Cola Kid." The bill under consideration involved wartime controls on sugar. Newspaper reporters pointed out that the Wisconsin Senator had struck up friendships with sugar lobbyists and officials of the Pepsi-Cola Company, who wanted sugar controls ended. During the Senate debate over the sugar bill, McCarthy tried to confuse colleagues by giving meaningless data and then misrepresenting the position of the Secretary of Agriculture. When a fellow Republican, Charles W. Tobey of New Hampshire, questioned the truthfulness of a McCarthy statement, the Wisconsin Senator replied that he did "not give a tinker's dam." He went on to accuse Tobey of introducing a "fictitious amendment" designed to "deceive" the public. Astounded at the charge, Senator Tobey accused McCarthy of "confusing the Senate of the United States." McCarthy finally succeeded in shortening the life of sugar rationing, but, more important, he revealed once again his willingness to distort facts and insult his Senate colleagues.

McCarthy fought like Indian Charlie in another Senate struggle over public housing. Joe's opposition to government-built housing led someone to call him "the water boy of the real estate lobby." In fact McCarthy did have close ties to private home builders and real estate interests who saw public housing as unfair competition. When McCarthy got on a committee to investigate public housing, he used a parliamentary technicality to deny the committee chairmanship to Senator Tobey, a supporter of public housing. This defied Senate custom, since Tobey was the senior member of the committee, and McCarthy's maneuver led Tobey to demand "straight shooting" in

24

committee proceedings. During the 1948 Senate battle over the housing bill, McCarthy helped defeat the public sections, and once again he personally attacked senators who disagreed with him.

McCarthy later raised Senate eyebrows when it came out that he had received $10,000 from the Lustron Corporation, a house builder. At the time Lustron made the payment, the company was under investigation by a Senate committee which included McCarthy. The check for $10,000 was supposedly in return for a 7,000-word pamphlet bearing McCarthy's name as author. This worked out to $1.43 a word, more than the record price paid to Winston Churchill for his World War II memoirs.

McCarthy's unsavory reputation made him an outcast among Senate insiders. When Democrats returned to control of the Senate in 1949, the new chairman of the Senate Banking Committee refused to serve if McCarthy kept his seat on the committee. "He's a troublemaker, that's why I don't want him," the committee chairman announced. Members of McCarthy's own party went along with this unusual request and banished McCarthy to the Committee on the District of Columbia, which senators considered the lowest possible assignment.

Increasingly disregarded by his colleagues, McCarthy turned to the Senate's investigating process to reap publicity. The object of McCarthy's attention was the so-called "Malmédy massacre." This World War II incident had occurred in December 1944, during a massive German offensive in which SS troops murdered hundreds of unarmed captives and local civilians in Belgium. Near the small town of Malmédy, Nazi troops machine-gunned to death 150 American prisoners of war. After the war, forty-three of the SS troopers were sentenced to death for their part in the Malmédy massacre. The former Nazi soldiers subsequently claimed that they had been forced to confess by torture and other extraordinary means. The result was a series of investigations, including one by the U.S. Senate in 1949.

The unpredictable Joe McCarthy emerged as a defender of the convicted SS soldiers. "Tail Gunner Joe" apparently took this strange position in part because of the large German population in Wisconsin and because several of his benefactors were pro-German businessmen. Furthermore, the Senator was probably once more looking for newspaper headlines.

McCarthy bluffed his way into the Senate's investigation of the Malmédy affair. After he threatened to start his own inquiry, he was permitted to sit in on the probe by a subcommittee of the Senate Armed Services Committee. The panel of three was chaired by Senator Raymond E. Baldwin, a Republican from Connecticut, but McCarthy dominated the proceedings. He bullied witnesses and shocked his colleagues with outrageous declarations. He called the American military judges in the Malmédy case "morons." "I think you are lying," he said to one witness. Finally, he insisted that the American interrogators and prosecutors of the convicted Nazis undergo lie-detector tests. When the Armed Services Committee rejected this suggestion, McCarthy stormed out, dismissing the hearings as "a shameful farce" and "a deliberate and clever attempt to whitewash the American military."

McCarthy continued his savage attacks against the committee and its chairman. In a Senate speech, he again called the Senate probe "a whitewash," and he charged that Senator Baldwin was "criminally responsible." This brought a demand from Senator Tobey that McCarthy be ruled out of order for a personal attack on a fellow senator. McCarthy, however, refused to back off, and his breach of

Senate ethics resulted in a rebuke from some of his colleagues. Both Republicans and Democrats on the Armed Services Committee issued a formal statement which praised Senator Baldwin for his "integrity, character and personality." The senators added, "We, his colleagues, take this unusual step in issuing this statement because of the most unusual, unfair, and utterly undeserved comments that have been made concerning Senator Baldwin."

McCarthy's ineffectiveness as a legislator and his outrageous conduct did not go unnoticed outside the Senate. By 1951 a poll of Washington reporters listed him as "the worst Senator" out of all ninety-six.

Aware that he was in political trouble, McCarthy began casting about for an issue that would insure his reelection in 1952. Early in 1950, he fixed his sights on the hottest issue of the time. He decided to ride the wave of anti-Communism which had been growing since the end of World War II and the increased Soviet domination of Eastern Europe.

3 | The "Red Menace"

American fears of Communism were at least as old as the Russian Revolution of 1917. The victorious Communists had adopted red as the color of their flag, and frightened Americans thought they saw the "red menace" wherever they looked. They worried not about a Soviet invasion, but about the threat within this country posed by radicals who favored extensive changes such as the abolition of private property. (Radicals are said to be on the political "left," and conservatives who oppose change are said to be on the "right.") Just as a small group of Bolsheviks had toppled the Russian government, so, too, a handful of Communists might overthrow the American government. Or at least that was what some Americans thought.

This fear of Communists taking over the United States was irrational, but very real. It rose during periods of stress, especially when strikes swept the country, and it subsided during years of relative social calm. In one sense, domestic Communists often served as scapegoats for economic and social problems, such as labor or racial unrest, that many confused Americans did not fully understand. The exaggerated fear of Communism also became a weapon in the hands of desperate politicans who falsely painted their opponents as "reds" or "pinks" allied with some Communist conspiracy.

The U.S. government sometimes fed the fear of domestic Communists. Almost as soon as the first Communist Party was formed in this country, the federal government took steps to deal with this supposedly "un-American" group. During the "Red Scare" of 1919–20, Woodrow Wilson's administration deported hundreds of noncitizens affiliated with the Communist movement. They were condemned not for any acts of violence, but rather for their beliefs and their membership in a party which preached the idea of revolution. In the years that followed, American leaders of the small Communist Party were jailed for allegedly plotting the overthrow of the government. To strong believers in free speech and a free press, this seemed a violation of constitutional guarantees, since the evidence against these radicals relied on their political activities and beliefs, not on any acts of violence. However, the Supreme Court upheld the government's crackdown.

Following World War I, the victims of the Red Scare included many people who were not even radicals, much less Communists. When non-Communist workers went on strike in Seattle during 1919, the city's mayor charged that local labor leaders wanted to "take possession of our American Government and try to duplicate the anarchy of Russia." After the strike collapsed, one Seattle newspaper declared, "This Bolshevik-sired nightmare is at an end."

Later that year when Boston policemen staged a walkout to get union recognition, local papers hysterically called the strike "a skirmish with Bolshevism" led by "agents of Lenin."

The first Red Scare came to an end in the early 1920s, but the fear of domestic Communism remained deeply imbedded in the minds of many Americans. The next outbreak of anti-Communism came in the 1930s, when conservative opponents of Franklin D. Roosevelt's New Deal tried to destroy moderate liberal programs, such as social security, by portraying them as Communistic. During the 1936 campaign, the Republican candidate for vice-president, Frank Knox, charged that Roosevelt had "been leading us toward Moscow." The anti–New Deal Hearst newspapers condemned:

> The Red New Deal with a Soviet seal
> Endorsed by a Moscow hand,
> The strange result of an alien cult
> In a liberty-loving land.

However, most Americans paid little attention to such ridiculous charges. Indeed, Roosevelt won reelection by a record margin in 1936.

However, in the late 1930s, resistance to the New Deal grew, and conservatives in Congress mounted a campaign to search for Communists in government. By 1938, the House of Representatives had created the Special Committee to Investigate Un-American Activities. Soon known as HUAC, the House Un-American Activities Committee was headed by Martin Dies, a Democrat from Texas who had turned against the New Deal. The Dies Committee investigated a variety of "un-American" groups such as the Ku Klux Klan and American Nazis, but it focused most of its efforts on the political left in general and Communists in particular.

The conservative members of HUAC zeroed in on the New Deal with vague charges that Communists and their sympathizers had infiltrated the federal government. "Stalin baited his hook with a 'progressive' worm, and the New Deal suckers swallowed bait, hook, line, and sinker," Dies claimed. Another Congressman on HUAC accused the Federal Theatre Project, a work-relief program for the unemployed, of producing plays "containing Communistic or New Deal theories."

The Dies Committee cast its net widely. Its attack on radicals was aimed not only at Communist Party members, who were in principle barred from federal employment under a 1939 law, but also at assorted leftists, liberals and others suspected of following the so-called "Communist line." These non–party members were branded "fellow travelers." Evidence to back up HUAC charges fell into a familiar pattern. The committee relied heavily on indirect links such as membership in left-wing groups or in so-called "Communist-front" organizations, which the Communist Party may have in fact dominated, or which may have only included some Communist Party members. Similarly, a person's friends or acquaintances could be pointed to as "proof" of his or her Communist tendencies. This process became known as "guilt by association," and HUAC frequently used it.

HUAC's "expert" witnesses were often themselves former Communist Party members. Some, such as Benjamin Gitlow, the party's 1924 candidate for Vice-President, had been high party officials. Despite their questionable backgrounds, these ex-Communists found that their word was accepted at face value when they testified before HUAC. The former Communists used the committee as a platform to confess the error of their previous ways and to give the names of those they remembered as having been involved in party activities.

The Dies Committee filled its reports with the names of supposedly "un-American" government employees. Most of the workers cited for suspicious activities were accused of rather vague left-wing tendencies, all of which—even if true—were perfectly legal. According to HUAC, 563 government workers were on the mailing list of the leftist American League for Peace and Democracy, 1,121 were "sympathetic with totalitarian ideology," and 72 had ties to the Political Action Committee of organized labor.

Despite its excesses, the Dies Committee proved popular. According to one public-opinion poll in 1938, three out of four people felt that the House Un-American Activities Committee should continue its work.

During World War II, HUAC received little notice. With the United States allied with the Soviet Union in the struggle against Nazi Germany, Americans showed less concern about Communists at home. After 1944, Martin Dies retired from Congress, but the following year HUAC was made a permanent congressional committee.

Postwar developments renewed American fears of the "red menace." By the end of World War II in 1945, the world had watched the Soviet Union take control of most of Eastern Europe and proceed to set up Communist governments in these occupied countries. This, combined with other sources of friction, destroyed the spirit of cooperation that had dominated Russian-American relations during World War II. Increased hostility soon led to the so-called "Cold War" between the U.S. and the Soviet Union. Although the two countries never engaged in actual warfare against each other, they confronted each other in a series of international crises.

The rise of the Cold War overseas was accompanied by a new Red Scare at home. Already distrustful of Communists, many Americans once again saw red after 1945.

Several incidents helped revive popular suspicions about possible Communist infiltration of the federal government.

In early 1945, federal agents secretly raided the offices of *Amerasia*, a small magazine devoted to Asian affairs. The discovery of a large number of classified State Department documents led to an FBI search for the source of this breach in security. On the basis of the FBI's investigation of the *Amerasia* case, the Justice Department obtained indictments against the magazine's two editors and a State Department employee. The three were charged with a conspiracy to steal confidential government documents. The Justice Department did not press charges of espionage because the purpose of the theft appeared to be publication of the documents, not their secret delivery to a foreign power. The government's case was also compromised by illegal searches for evidence, which the defendants soon learned about. As a result, the Justice Department settled for small fines of two defendants in order to avoid a jury trial.

However, the *Amerasia* case could not be disposed of so easily. For congressmen frightened of a supposed Communist conspiracy, the *Amerasia* incident was proof that the government would not take effective action against spies. One congressman called the handling of the case a "whitewash" and an "open invitation to sabotage," engineered by the "left-wing crowd" in the government. The upshot was a 1946 congressional probe of the entire affair. The investigators finally concluded that despite evidence of weak security measures, there was no reason to criticize the government's handling of the case. Nevertheless, *Amerasia* became a code word for people convinced that Communism represented a real threat within the United States.

Other evidence of a spy network came from Canadian revelations in 1946 that the Russians had engaged in extensive espionage in that country. Although this was hardly proof that Communists infested the U.S. Government, anti-administration politicians gave voters that impression.

During the 1946 election campaign, Republicans appealed to rising fears of Communism. The head of the Republican National Committee charged that "red-Fascists" who were "beholden to the political ideology of Moscow" had captured control of the Democratic Party. Another Republican spokesman pledged that his party would end "boring from within by subversionists high up in government." In part because of the Communist issue, Republicans won control of Congress in the 1946 election.

Faced with pressures at home and abroad, President Harry S. Truman announced an anti-Communist crusade in 1947. Truman had become President upon Roosevelt's death in 1945. As Chief Executive, he gradually built an image as a tough, decisive man who would tackle any challenge; on his White House desk sat a plaque with the motto "The Buck Stops Here." In March 1947, Truman announced that the U.S. would seek to contain any further expansion of the Soviet Union overseas. Defending this new foreign policy, he denounced Communism as the mortal enemy of the American way of life.

Truman's initiative in foreign policy was coupled with a crackdown on domestic Communists. In March 1947 he issued Executive Order 9835 establishing the Federal Employee Loyalty Program, which was designed to investigate the loyalty of all present and future government workers. Possible grounds for dismissal included not only Communist Party membership, but also, in Truman's words, "membership in, affiliation with, or sympathetic

34

association with any foreign or domestic organization . . . designated by the Attorney General as totalitarian, fascist, communist or subversive."

In addition to rooting out possible subversives in government, the Truman administration launched a drive to deport aliens associated with Communism, and it moved to prosecute American leaders of the Communist Party. President Truman thus made "internal security" a top priority in the midst of the Cold War.

If Truman's goal was to defuse the Communist issue through his various actions, he failed. If anything, he only fueled the growing national hysteria by exaggerating the threat of internal subversion. As a result, he gave his political enemies additional ammunition to use against the administration. Indeed, some historians have accused President Truman of sowing the seeds of McCarthyism.

In their effort to dislodge Democrats from power, Republicans again seized on the Communist issue. Although this was not dominant in the 1948 campaign, some anti-Communist rhetoric was used against Truman and the Democrats. The Republican national chairman predicted that a GOP victory would bring "the greatest housecleaning . . . since Saint Patrick cleaned the snakes out of Ireland." Thomas E. Dewey, the party's presidential candidate, promised, "There will not be any Communists in the Government after January 20." Dewey's running mate, Earl Warren, accused the administration of "coddling" Communists.

President Truman resorted to similar rhetoric to prove he was not soft on Communism. Pointing to his foreign policy of containment and his internal-security program, Truman argued that the Communists "wanted a Republican victory." He suggested that voters "consider well the strange bedfellows the Republican Party has this year."

Truman and the Democrats won a surprise victory in 1948. This upset seemed to make Republicans even more desperate in their desire to regain the power they had lost in 1932.

While Truman was putting together his internal-security program during 1947-48, Congress also had shown greater concern with subversion. Although a number of House and Senate committees hunted for subversives across the country, the House Un-American Activities Committee continued to command the most attention. Under Republican leadership, HUAC sought "to expose and ferret out the communists and communist sympathizers in the federal government." HUAC's relentless search led it to demand that the Truman administration turn over the confidential loyalty files of government employees. The President refused, thereby igniting a new controversy.

Without access to loyalty files, HUAC still relied heavily on the testimony of former Communists. After years of digging around in the past of disillusioned radicals, the committee finally hit pay dirt in 1948, when Whittaker Chambers publicly accused nine former government officials of membership in the Communist Party. Chambers, then a senior editor of *Time* magazine, admitted having been a secret agent doing espionage for the Communist Party for a period up to 1938. Chambers' most explosive charge centered on Alger Hiss, who, according to Chambers, had been a close friend and fellow Communist during the 1930s. Hiss, a Harvard Law School graduate, had held several positions in the Roosevelt administration before ending up in the State Department, where he had served until his resignation from the government in 1946.

At first, Chambers' charge against Hiss appeared to have little foundation. Hiss went before HUAC and denied ever having been a Communist. A number of Democrats and high State Department officials stepped forward to vouch for the integrity of Alger Hiss. President Truman called the charge a "red herring." When Whittaker Chambers repeated his accusation in a radio interview, Hiss sued Chambers for slander, charging that the former Communist had made "untrue, false and defamatory" accusations.

As the pressure on Chambers increased, he expanded his charges against Hiss to include espionage. Chambers produced copies of State Department documents from the 1930s that he claimed to have received from Hiss. (The microfilm had been temporarily hidden in a hollowed-out pumpkin on Chambers' farm and hence became known as the "Pumpkin Papers.") On the basis of this evidence, a federal grand jury indicted Alger Hiss in December 1948. Under the statute of limitations, the crime of espionage during peacetime can be prosecuted only within three years after it was committed, so Hiss was charged instead with two counts of perjury for allegedly having lied under oath when he said that he had neither seen Chambers after 1937 nor passed government documents to him.

Long-drawn-out court proceedings followed. The first trial of Hiss for perjury ended with the jury unable to agree on a verdict. A second trial produced a finding of guilty in January 1950, and Hiss was sentenced to five years in federal prison.

The conviction of Alger Hiss did not end the controversy surrounding the case. His defenders claimed that he had been railroaded by insufficient or doctored evidence. However, for those Americans terrified by the specter of a Communist conspiracy haunting the government, the conviction of Hiss seemed proof that their suspicions were correct. In the 1950s his name became a byword for the charge that Communist spies infested the federal government. People who believed this overlooked the fact that the Hiss case was the only case that produced a conviction related in any way to espionage in Washington, and that the case concerned events that had occurred in the 1930s, not the Cold War years. (In March 1950 a Justice Department employee, Judith Coplon, was found guilty of passing secrets to the Soviets, but an appeals court overturned the conviction because the government had secured evidence illegally.)

Several events in 1949 had served to increase fears of Communists. Americans already disturbed by signs of Soviet aggressiveness were shocked in September 1949 to learn that the Soviets had successfully tested their first atomic bomb. For the first time Americans began to grapple with the thought that an unfriendly foreign power could unleash a devastating atomic attack that could destroy the United States.

In December 1949, three months after the Russians exploded their first A-bomb, Americans received news of another Communist breakthrough. This one came in the Far East, where Chinese Communist forces finally won complete control of mainland China. This struggle had been under way for years, but the sudden reality of "Red China" dramatically added to American apprehensions.

As the "red menace" loomed ever larger overseas, evidence of the internal threat mounted in the winter of 1949–50. During October 1949, eleven leaders of the American Communist Party were found guilty of conspiring to overthrow the government of the U.S. Although this was a narrow charge that did not encompass any overt acts of violence, it did nothing to calm the fears of nervous Americans. On the heels of this trial had come the conviction of Alger Hiss in January 1950. Then, on February 4, news reached the United States that the British had arrested a nuclear physicist, Klaus Fuchs, on charges of spying for the Russians. Fuchs, it was revealed, had previously worked at an American atomic laboratory, and a week after his arrest he confessed to having engaged in espionage during his years in the U.S.

Republicans moved quickly to use these developments for partisan purposes. On February 6, 1950, GOP leaders adopted a statement attacking "the dangerous degree to which Communists and their fellow travelers have been employed in important Government posts and the fact that information vital to our security has been made available to alien agents and persons of questionable loyalty." Republicans denounced the "soft attitude of this Administration toward Government employees and officials who hold or support Communist attitudes."

As the public hysteria and partisan atmosphere heated up, Joe McCarthy was looking for an issue that might win him reelection in 1952. On January 7, 1950, at a now famous "Dinner at the Colony"—Washington's Colony Restaurant—he consulted with Father Edmund A. Walsh, dean of the School of Foreign Service at Georgetown University; Charles H. Kraus, an instructor of political science at Georgetown and a McCarthy assistant; and William A. Roberts, a Washington attorney. The four bounced around ideas for McCarthy to focus on. Roberts suggested the St. Lawrence Seaway that was designed to link Wisconsin and other midwestern states to the Atlantic Ocean through the Great Lakes. McCarthy tossed out this idea, but brought up the possibility of an improved pension plan for the elderly. However, his listeners turned it down. As the conversation dragged on, someone suggested the issue of Communism.

"The government is full of Communists," McCarthy reportedly exclaimed: "The thing to do is hammer at them."

The three other men immediately cautioned that an anti-Communist campaign would require facts to back up charges; otherwise, the cry of "reds" would add up to nothing more than the cry of "wolf" by the little boy who screamed it so often that no one listened.

Asked in April 1950 how long ago he had found the issue of Communism, McCarthy replied, "Two and a half months." This would date the origins to the January meeting at the Colony, but, like many politicians, McCarthy had occasionally resorted to anti-Communist rhetoric during the late 1940s. In his 1946 senatorial campaign he had used it in passing. His opposition to public housing led him in 1947 to call one project a "breeding ground for Communism." In October 1949 he suggested that some State Department personnel might be "more sympathetic to certain foreign ideologies than to our own." The following month he charged that an opposition Wisconsin newspaper was "the red mouthpiece for the Communist Party in Wisconsin."

These outbursts prior to 1950 attracted no notice because they were sufficiently vague and infrequent. Moreover, they were pretty standard fare for the times.

However, once Joe McCarthy latched onto the issue of Communism in government, he showed a remarkable ability to outdistance other politicians who had emphasized "redbaiting" long before him. Taking full advantage of the anti-Communist hysteria that had been building for some time, he launched his new career during the Lincoln Day speeches of 1950.

4 | The Speech Heard Round the World

Abraham Lincoln is the patron saint of the Republican Party. His birthday annually provides Republicans with an opportunity to sing the praises of their party. By a happy coincidence this mid-February ritual comes just at the time politicians gear up for November elections. Thus Republican speakers frequently use the occasion to fire the first shots of the upcoming election campaign.

Bookings for Lincoln's Birthday speeches are a good measure of power and influence in Republican circles. The most prominent party leaders draw the choice cities where the largest audiences are expected. Lesser lights are assigned to smaller out-of-the-way places.

On February 9, 1950, Senator Joe McCarthy found himself speaking before the Ohio County Women's Republican Club in Wheeling, West Virginia. With only three years' experience in the U.S. Senate, McCarthy was little known outside his home state of Wisconsin, and he undoubtedly had limited aspirations in Wheeling. In addition to reaching his local West Virginia audience, McCarthy could at best have hoped that his remarks might be picked up by newspapers in Wisconsin.

Using excerpts from prior speeches of more famous Republicans, McCarthy spoke on the topic of Communism. After charting the course of the Cold War, he argued that the U.S. and the Soviet Union were "engaged in a showdown fight . . . between two diametrically opposed ideologies." The great moral conflict pitted "our Western Christian world" against "the atheistic Communist world." Declaring, "The chips are down—they are truly down," the Senator contended that the U.S. was losing the ideological battle with Russia.

Pacing the platform and waving his arms for emphasis, McCarthy then gave his explanation of the cause of American defeats in the Cold War. "The reason why we find ourselves in a position of impotency is not because our only powerful potential enemy has sent men to invade our shores, but rather because of the traitorous actions of those who have been treated so well by this nation." The chief villains were "those who have had all the benefits that the wealthiest nation on earth has had to offer—the finest homes, the finest college education, and the finest jobs in Government we can give. This is glaringly true in the State Department. There the bright young men who are born with silver spoons in their mouths are the ones who have been the worst." The Senator went on to give the names of four State Department employees who had supposedly betrayed the United States in their handling of American foreign policy.

McCarthy then made his most explosive charge, but his exact words are a subject of dispute. According to the sworn statement of two newsmen, the Senator picked up a piece of paper and said,

> While I cannot take the time to name all of the men in the State Department who have been named as members of the Communist Party and members of a spy ring, I have here in my hand a list of 205—a list of names that were made known to the Secretary of State and who nevertheless are still working and shaping the policy of the State Department.

Did this really mean that there were 205 known Communist spies in the State Department? McCarthy left his Wheeling audience with that impression. However, he called not for arrests and prosecutions but for a "moral uprising" to sweep "the whole sorry mess of twisted, warped thinkers ... from the national scene so that we may have a new birth of national honesty and decency in Government."

Senator McCarthy's speech on Communism in government initially received little attention. Except for the Chicago *Tribune,* no major newspaper printed the Associated Press story which carried the reference to "a list of 205."

However, as McCarthy's speaking tour continued westward, publicity increased after reporters pressed the Senator for clarification. Typically, he chose to muddy the waters that swirled around him. While changing planes in Denver on February 10, he made a show of looking for his list of Communists in the State Department and then told reporters he had left it on the plane. By the time McCarthy arrived in Salt Lake City later that day, he had begun to hedge in statements to the press. He said the list of 205 referred to "bad risks" in the State Department. However, he added that he knew of fifty-seven "card-carrying Communists" working in the State Department. He produced neither list.

On a radio show that evening he offered to turn over the names of Communist employees to the Secretary of State. "Now, I want to tell the Secretary this: If he wants to call me tonight at the Utah Hotel, I will be glad to give him the names of those fifty-seven card-carrying Communists." In a more sweeping statement, he added, "I don't want to indicate there are only fifty-seven, I say I have the names of fifty-seven."

The following day, February 11, McCarthy traveled to Reno, Nevada, for another Lincoln's Birthday address. The rough draft handed out in advance to newsmen had the number 205 scratched out and the number 57 added. McCarthy hedged still further when he told his Reno audience, "I have in my hand fifty-seven cases of individuals who would appear to be either card-carrying members or certainly loyal to the Communist Party but who nevertheless are still helping to shape our foreign policy."

From Reno, McCarthy also fired off a telegram to President Harry S. Truman. The Republican Senator challenged the Democratic President to give Congress the names of all the people in the State Department listed as "bad security risks because of their communistic connections." McCarthy added in a threatening tone, "Failure on your part will label the Democratic Party of being the bedfellow of international communism."

The Truman administration dismissed McCarthy's charges. At a press conference, the President flatly stated there "was not a word of truth in what the Senator said." A spokesman for the State Department declared, "We know of no Communist party members in the department, and if we find any they will be summarily dismissed." Referring to the list of names mentioned repeatedly by McCarthy, the State Department official asserted, "We would be interested in seeing his list." The Senator disregarded all requests for a copy of the list he claimed to possess. (Asked privately at a later date what he had held in his hand at Wheeling, McCarthy impishly replied, "An old laundry list.")

The newest controversy surrounding Joe McCarthy had begun. *The New York Times* compared him to a hit-and-run driver who leaves behind a trail of victims. McCarthy's conflicting statements also left a number of unanswered questions. Did he have any list at all? If so, how many names did it contain? Two hundred and five? Fifty-seven? Who were these people? Were they "card-carrying Communists," "loyal to the Communist Party" or simply "bad risks"? Were they still State Department employees?

5 | The Senate Investigates

Senator Joe McCarthy was in the national spotlight when he returned to Washington from his whirlwind speaking tour for Lincoln's Birthday. Following his blanket charge that "card-carrying Communists" worked in the State Department, the public anxiously waited for McCarthy to drop the other shoe by proving his accusation. Indeed, some newspaper editorials demanded that the Senator "put up or shut up."

On February 20, 1950, eleven days after his Wheeling speech, McCarthy took to the floor of the U.S. Senate to explain his charges. Arriving late in the afternoon with a bulging briefcase supposedly filled with evidence, he launched into an eight-hour performance that showed he would lie repeatedly to make his case.

In the attempt to explain the shifting number of subversives he had referred to, McCarthy only added to the confusion. He pointed out that the number 205 came from a 1946 letter in which the Secretary of State had told Congress that the State Department had screened about 3,000 employees transferred to the department from other agencies. Of these the department had recommended against permanent employment for 285 for a variety of reasons, and 79 of the individuals had already been let go. Four years later, McCarthy subtracted 79 from 285 and came up with the number 205. His logic was even worse than his arithmetic. The negative findings of the State Department had been based on a number of reasons, not only security considerations, and many of the "205" no longer worked for the government by 1950. But newsmen in Wheeling had heard the Senator turn all 205 into "members of the Communist Party" who were "still working" in the State Department.

However, in his Senate speech McCarthy once again backed away from the number 205. Admitting he did not have a written text in Wheeling, he nevertheless read to his fellow senators the speech he now claimed to have made in West Virginia. In this version he referred to "fifty-seven cases of individuals who would appear to be either card-carrying members or certainly loyal to the Communist Party." Thus he not only reduced the number but also softened the charge to include loyalty to the Communist Party.

Having apparently fixed on the number 57, McCarthy again shifted his ground. With the announcement that he had penetrated "Truman's iron curtain of secrecy," the Senator declared that he would present the facts from eighty-one cases, thus introducing a third magic number. McCarthy left his colleagues with the distinct impression that this was fresh information taken directly from State Department files by "some good, loyal Americans." In fact it turned out that the eighty-one cases of unnamed persons

47

were from State Department records that congressional investigators had received in 1947. At that time fifty-seven of the individuals were actually State Department employees, and the information against them, much of it based on rumor, included allegations of everything from Communist Party membership to homosexuality.

In McCarthy's hands these old files became evidence "of the number of Communists in the State Department." However, even he was forced to admit that not all of the eighty-one were State Department employees in 1950. "I may say that I know that some of these individuals whose cases I am giving the Senate are no longer in the State Department," he confessed in a moment of candor. "A sizeable number of them are not." Some, it turned out, were not even suspect according to the Senator. He personally described one of the eighty-one as "a good, loyal American."

Reverting to his more familiar style, McCarthy pretended to summarize the records of the list of eighty-one. In the process he so twisted the evidence that it often bore little resemblance to the original. One case had no information except age and place of employment. In McCarthy's version, the individual became "a known Communist." The Senator described a job applicant never hired by the State Department as "still in the Department as of today." In short, McCarthy tried to prove his charges by distorting outdated information that had been in the hands of Congress for three years.

Despite his use of untruths and half-truths, Senator McCarthy went largely unchallenged by his unsuspecting colleagues. Democratic senators freqently interrupted him in the attempt to pin down his numbers and to get him to name names, yet who among McCarthy's opponents could guess that a U.S. senator would simply lie?

After all, the Senate was held up as the greatest deliberative body in the world, and McCarthy, although abrasive and even rude, was a member of that highly respected body. As long as he played by the rules, or at least did not stretch them too far, McCarthy was safe. One rule also protected him from his victims. Congressional immunity prevents anyone from suing a senator for statements made on the floor of Congress. The Wisconsin Senator told his colleagues that he would resign if he ever refused to repeat outside anything he said before the Senate. Nevertheless, McCarthy carefully avoided saying anything outside the Senate chamber that might result in a libel suit testing his truthfulness.

Although few senators heard McCarthy's performance on February 20, those present made it clear that reactions to McCarthy would generally follow party lines. On the one hand, fellow Republicans helped McCarthy present his evidence by asking friendly questions and running interference when Democrats tried to sidetrack him. Republicans also praised McCarthy's efforts to root out Communists; on the other hand, a few Democrats continually interrupted the Wisconsin Senator and challenged his statements. However, Democrats could not afford to block an investigation of McCarthy's charges, because that would open them to the additional charge of trying to cover up the alleged presence of Communists in government.

On the following day, the Senate's Democratic majority took the bull by the horns and called for a formal investigation. As drafted by the Democratic leadership, Senate Resolution 231 authorized the Committee on Foreign Relations "to conduct a full and complete study as to whether persons who are disloyal to the United States are employed by the Department of State as charged by the

Senator from Wisconsin (Mr. McCarthy)." Republicans immediately objected to the narrowness of the resolution, arguing that the investigation should not be limited to McCarthy's charges. Moreover, Republicans wanted the committee to have access to loyalty files which President Truman had refused since 1948 to turn over to Congress. Democrats countered that McCarthy should give the sources of his information. The Wisconsin Senator said flatly that he would never reveal the name of any government informant, because "that man's job would not be worth a tinker's dam."

In the highly charged political atmosphere, the Democratic majority accepted Republican revisions, and Resolution 231 passed unanimously. As amended, the resolution called on the Foreign Relations Committee for "a full and complete study" of possible disloyalty on the part of present or past employees of the State Department. The committee was also directed to examine employee loyalty files.

Claiming they had nothing to hide, State Department officials welcomed the investigation. Secretary of State Dean Acheson pointed out to reporters, "There is now no one in the Department who has been found to be disloyal by the President's Loyalty Board, or who has been held to be a bad security risk." However, Acheson added that, since questions had been raised, the department was "glad to have the opportunity to show the Congress, and through it the people, that effective steps have been and are being taken to guarantee that the department is staffed only by persons loyal to the country."

Toward the end of February 1950 the Senate Foreign Relations Committee put its inquiry into the hands of a five-man subcommittee. This specially created group was composed of three Democratic senators and two Republicans. Headed by Senator Millard E. Tydings, a Democrat from Maryland, the investigating body became known as the Tydings Committee. Its chairman looked as if he had been picked by a Hollywood casting director. A tall, trim blue-eyed gentleman, Tydings was an excellent debater who could destroy a political opponent with devastating rhetoric and biting wit. The other Democrats on the committee were Brien McMahon of Connecticut and Theodore Green of Rhode Island. The Republicans were Henry Cabot Lodge, Jr., of Massachusetts and Bourke Hickenlooper of Iowa.

Senator Tydings clearly had been selected by the Democratic leadership to look out for party interests. After all, the pending investigation would look into Republican charges that the Democratic-controlled State Department employed Communists. Political sensibilities were further aroused by the common knowledge that the committee's findings could affect the outcome of the 1950 and 1952 elections for Congress and the 1952 presidential election.

The Tydings Committee began its public hearings on March 8 in a circus atmosphere. Expecting a good show, spectators lined up early for prized seats in the Senate Caucus Room. The proceedings were literally in the spotlight of newsmen gathered to capture the drama on film. The first witness was the junior Senator from Wisconsin who had started the furor. Several years later, McCarthy recalled his thoughts as he entered the hearing room.

"In the back of my mind," McCarthy wrote, "there was faintly echoing the chairman's statement, 'Let me have McCarthy for three days in public hearings and he will never show his face in the Senate again.'" (Senator Tydings denied he ever said any such thing, but it fit McCarthy's image of himself as the fighter, single-handedly taking on the entire federal government.)

"It was to be a contest," according to McCarthy, "between a lone Senator and all the vast power of the federal bureaucracy pin-pointed in and backing up the Tydings Committee." Then, resorting to a half-truth, McCarthy added, "The picture of treason which I carried in my briefcase to that Caucus room was to shock the nation and occupy the headlines until Truman declared war in Korea." The picture of treason was a creation of McCarthy's imagination, but the headlines he got were very real.

When McCarthy tried to read a prepared statement to the Tydings Committee, the decorum of the Senate Caucus Room was quickly shattered. Senator Tydings interrupted with a demand that the witness give the names of several people he had accused. McCarthy refused. In a show of party unity, Republican committee members defended McCarthy's right to proceed as he wished. The bickering so delayed the hearing that McCarthy barely had time to begin reading his statement before the committee adjourned for the day. But McCarthy did not care. He already had insured that he would capture newspaper headlines, by releasing the full text of his statement before testifying. And even in that short space of time he was able to name his first name since the Wheeling speech a month earlier.

The first case brought up by McCarthy was typical of the many which followed. He charged that Dorothy Kenyon was a State Department employee who had been "affiliated with at least twenty-eight Communist-front organizations." Embellishing this accusation, McCarthy added that "the Communist activities of Miss Kenyon" were "not only deep-rooted but extend back through the years." As proof the Senator read from lists of sponsors of a number of left-wing organizations. In the process he linked the name of Dorothy Kenyon to "well-known Communists."

When she learned of this, Kenyon called McCarthy "an unmitigated liar." She also dared the Senator to repeat his charges outside the Senate so that he could be sued for slander. When McCarthy refused, Kenyon dismissed him as "a coward to take shelter in the cloak of Congressional immunity."

Here was a case where McCarthy's charges could be immediately tested against the known facts. Dorothy Kenyon was a lawyer and former New York City judge who had a record as a liberal New Deal Democrat. She had in fact been associated in a variety of ways, such as signing protest statements, with numerous groups, some of which had Communist as well as non-Communist members. Six of these organizations had been labeled as so-called "Communist fronts" by the Attorney General, but Kenyon's association with all had ended *before* the government listed them as suspect. Furthermore, Kenyon had never worked directly for the State Department, much less influenced U.S. foreign policy. The closest she came was a 1947 appointment to the United Nations Commission on the Status of Women, and she had completed her UN work the year before McCarthy attacked her.

When the sixty-two-year-old woman demanded that she be given the right to respond under oath to McCarthy's charges, the Senator showed less interest in her. He failed even to attend when she testified before the Tydings Committee. Kenyon's emotional and convincing recital of her past record concluded with the statement "There is not a Communist bone in my body!" The lone Republican Senator present asked a few questions and then declared there was no evidence that Dorothy Kenyon had been "in any way subversive or disloyal."

In addition to attacking Dorothy Kenyon, McCarthy made charges against eight other individuals in his long opening statement to the Tydings Committee. Far from accusing these people of being "card-carrying" Communist Party members, McCarthy settled for the sweeping, but vague, charge that all had "communist affiliations."As in the case of Kenyon, this added up to little upon close inspection, but it could be made to appear very damaging, especially since McCarthy relied on the tactic of hit-and-run, refusing to confront any of his victims.

The basic method employed by Senator McCarthy in his hunt for Communists remained much the same over the next few years. Repeatedly, by linking various people, many of them not even government employees, to left-wing groups that may also have had Communist members or been branded as "Communist fronts," he tried to prove that Communists had infiltrated the government. This was the familiar technique of "guilt by association" —that is, judging people not by what they did but by their affiliations, however vague those might be. By the time the truth could catch up with McCarthy's accusations, reputations were frequently destroyed and careers ruined.

Senator McCarthy employed this destructive political method so often that it quickly became known as "McCarthyism." The term came to mean, according to *The Random House Dictionary*, "public accusation of disloyalty . . . in many instances unsupported by proof or based on slight, doubtful, or irrelevant evidence." In an early-1950 cartoon, artist Herbert Block ("Herblock") depicted McCarthyism by putting the word on barrels of mud that were stacked high and ready to fall in any direction.

Whenever the truth caught up with one of McCarthy's charges, he had usually moved on to other, supposedly more important, cases. For example, when McCarthy's first cases added up to nothing, he suddenly announced to the press on March 21, 1950, that he would name "the top Russian espionage agent" in the United States. Then

McCarthy delayed giving reporters the spy's name, in an effort to milk this sensational revelation for all it was worth. Senator Tydings immediately called a subcommittee meeting to pursue this latest and most mysterious charge. In a closed session, McCarthy revealed the name, but he added, "There is nothing mysterious about this one." In fact, the person turned out to be someone already mentioned by McCarthy in his first nine cases presented to the Tydings Committee. Now, however, he singled out the case as "explosive." "If you crack this case," he argued, "it will be the biggest espionage case in the history of this country." Refusing to provide any additional evidence, McCarthy concluded, "I am willing to stand or fall on this one. If I am shown to be wrong on this, I think the subcommittee would be justified in not taking my other cases too seriously."

Reporters soon learned from McCarthy that he was referring to Owen Lattimore, a university scholar who was an expert on Asia. Many Americans who had been surprised by the Communist takeover of China in 1949 were prepared to believe that Communists in the U.S. State Department had committed treason to help the Chinese Communists triumph. However, Professor Lattimore was neither a Communist nor an employee of the State Department. Instead, he was a private citizen who had worked for the Office of War Information during World War II and then served briefly as a government consultant in 1949. Informed of McCarthy's charges, Lattimore called them "pure moonshine."

After winning headlines with his initial accusation against Lattimore, McCarthy began to waffle. In a four-hour speech to the Senate on March 30, he described Lattimore as a "bad policy risk" and "the architect of our Far Eastern policy." This, of course, was not illegal, let alone proof that Lattimore was a spy. McCarthy himself admitted, "I fear in the case of Lattimore, I may have perhaps placed too much stress on the question of whether or not he has been an espionage agent." The Senator promised, however, to produce a witness who would swear that Lattimore had been a Communist Party member.

Giving McCarthy a good dose of his own medicine, Owen Lattimore branded the Senator a "base and miserable creature" and a "hit-and-run politician." Lattimore added, "No one likes to be splattered with mud, even by a madman." Early in April, Lattimore testified publicly before the Tydings Committee, and he denied all the charges against himself. Furthermore, he looked straight at his accuser and denounced the "reign of terror" produced by "the machine gun of irresponsible publicity in Joseph McCarthy's hands."

At the conclusion of Lattimore's testimony, Senator Tydings announced that committee members had reviewed a summary of the professor's loyalty file. According to Tydings, there was "nothing in the files to show that you have ever been a Communist or have been connected with espionage."

In response McCarthy exclaimed to reporters, "Either Tydings hasn't seen the files or he is lying."

Drawn-out hearings on the Lattimore case continued through April. The string of witnesses included Communists and former Communists who contradicted each other. One ex-Communist said he was once told that Lattimore was a party member. However, another former Communist dismissed this statement as laughable. Out of the conflicting testimony about Lattimore came no proof that he had ever been a Communist or a spy.

Despite the failure to prove his charges against

Lattimore—or any of the others he had named—McCarthy continued to gain momentum during the spring of 1950. He was a master at exploiting the news media, most of which uncritically reported his every charge. Newspapers thrived on scoops and sensational stories which the Wisconsin Senator readily supplied just in time for press deadlines. When the evidence—or lack of it—began to contradict one of McCarthy's charges, he simply shifted his ground or moved on to another case. For example, the first explosive charge against the unnamed Owen Lattimore had resulted in the following *New York Times* headline: "CHIEF 'RUSSIAN SPY' NAMED BY M'CARTHY." As the number of startling accusations and sensational headlines multiplied, many newspaper readers must have increasingly believed that there was some truth in what Senator McCarthy said even if the evidence failed to support an individual case. After all, where there was so much smoke, surely there must be a bright red fire.

In editorial columns some newspapers criticized the Senator's failure to back up his charges. The Louisville *Courier-Journal* accused him of engaging in a "fishing expedition" which "borders on the outrageous." The Denver *Post* condemned his "branding individuals without evidence" and declared that "such inexcusable irresponsibility makes Americans wish the laws of libel and slander applied to utterances on the Senate floor." According to a newspaper editorial in his home state, McCarthy was "willing to ruin the lives of innocent people" in order to "satisfy his own craving for headlines." Despite the frequency of these attacks on McCarthy's methods, they appeared on the inside editorial pages which were reserved for opinions. Meanwhile, McCarthy occupied the front pages which were supposedly places of fact and hard news.

McCarthy also effectively sidestepped the widespread demand that he prove his charges about Communism in government. He simply responded that the proof was buried in loyalty investigation files of the State Department and that it was up to the Tydings Committee to get access to the records. However, in a 1948 executive order President Truman had closed these files to Congress. Truman's position was that the raw files contained hearsay and gossip that might injure the reputations of persons who had been investigated but found to be loyal. Furthermore, disclosure of the files might reveal FBI sources of information. For these reasons, FBI Director J. Edgar Hoover publicly supported the President's refusal to turn over loyalty files. Although this position was understandable, McCarthy painted it in the worst possible light.

"It is up to the President to put up or shut up," McCarthy declared. "Unless the President is afraid of what the files would disclose he should hand them over."

Recognizing that withholding the files smacked of a cover-up, Democratic senators pressured Truman to release the records. Apparently prepared to take this course, the President agreed, but he set certain conditions. In May 1950, Senator Tydings announced that the President would let subcommittee members examine the files. However, senators had to look at the files in the White House, and they could not take any notes.

The compromise did not satisfy McCarthy, who said the files were "not tamper proof." Indeed, when the Tydings Committee found nothing in the records to prove McCarthy's charges, the Senator simply declared that the loyalty files had been "raped."

Stung by McCarthy's barbs, Democrats increasingly responded in similar fashion. The President himself stated in a March press conference that the Wisconsin Senator was "the greatest asset that the Kremlin has." By May, Democratic senators had also begun to pull off their gloves. One called McCarthy "a very talented propagandist of the Soviet type." Such outbursts testified to the growing fear among Democrats that McCarthy was winning the battle of words. One frustrated Democrat commented privately, "The answers so far have plainly not caught up with the charges."

Sensing they could make political hay out of the Communist issue, some leading Republicans formed a chorus of support behind McCarthy. The Republican national chairman credited members of his party with exposing the fact that "spies, emissaries, agents and members of the Communist party . . . infest the Government of the United States." Senator Robert A. Taft of Ohio, looking forward to the 1950 elections, said that McCarthy's charges were "not a matter of party policy," but he personally urged the Wisconsin Senator to "keep talking and if one case doesn't work, bring up another."

Not all Republicans lined up behind McCarthy. On June 1, 1950, six moderate Republicans joined in support of Senator Margaret Chase Smith, who issued what she called a "Declaration of Conscience." Speaking, she said, as a Republican, a woman, a senator and an American, Mrs. Smith declared that the U.S. Senate had recently "been debased to the level of a forum of hate and character assassination sheltered by the shield of congressional immunity." Although she did not mention Joseph McCarthy by name, she made it clear she was directing her remarks at the Republican Senator from Wisconsin. "I am not proud," she observed, "of the reckless abandon in which unproved charges have been hurled from this [Republican] side of the aisle." She concluded, "There are enough mistakes of the Democrats for Republicans to criticize constructively without resorting to political smears."

As the debate over McCarthy's tactics heated up, the Tydings Committee completed its investigation. After almost four months of hearings, the committee Democrats voted to call a halt and report their findings. The Republican minority sought in vain to continue the inquiry. The five Tydings Committee members also divided along party lines in the final report issued on July 17, 1950. The Democrats, who were the majority, accused McCarthy of perpetrating "a fraud and a hoax" and "perhaps the most nefarious campaign of half-truths and untruth in the history of this Republic." The majority on the committee also found that "the charges made by Senator McCarthy were groundless and that the Senate and the American people had been deceived." The full Senate adopted the final report by a strict party vote, with the Democratic majority pushing it through. Republicans dismissed the findings as a "scandalous and brazen whitewash of treasonable conspiracy." McCarthy attacked the report as "a signal to the traitors, Communists, and fellow travelers in our Government that they need have no fear of exposure."

Thus ended the first round in the fight over McCarthyism. The Tydings Committee had not resolved the issue of Communism in government. Instead, the investigation had widened the split between Republicans and Democrats and confirmed that the debate would largely follow party lines. Furthermore, the Tydings Committee had generated more publicity for McCarthy and helped make his name a household word.

6 | McCarthyism at Work

McCarthyism was a product of the times. In the wake of Truman's loyalty program, the Russians' explosion of an atomic bomb, the takeover of China by the Communists, and the conviction of Alger Hiss, confused Americans were prepared to believe that foreign-policy reversals were the result of a Communist conspiracy within the federal government. In June 1950, American fears were further aroused by the outbreak of the Korean War.

Korea, a small Asian country bordering on China, had been occupied by the United States and the Soviet Union after World War II, the Americans occupying the southern part and the Soviets the northern. In their zone of North Korea, the Soviets had helped put Communists in power. Meanwhile in South Korea, the Americans had supported a government friendly to the United States. By 1950, both the U.S. and the Soviet Union had withdrawn their troops from Korea, but their departure left two hostile Korean governments facing each other across the 38th parallel, which divided the country.

On June 25, 1950, Communist North Korea invaded South Korea. President Truman immediately sent military aid to the South Koreans. When this failed to halt the advancing Communists, Truman ordered U.S. troops to Korea under a United Nations resolution that also brought token support from several other countries. American intervention steadily forced the North Koreans to retreat until they reached the 38th parallel in October. At that point the United States decided to go for a complete victory by crossing the 38th parallel and pushing into North Korea. Within a few weeks U.S. and South Korean troops had successfully fought through North Korea, and some reached the country's border with China. The Chinese Communists then launched an assault that quickly reversed the military situation. By the end of 1950, the Americans were retreating and facing defeat in the Korean War.

Republicans wasted no time in criticizing Truman's handling of the Korean War. With congressional elections approaching in November, the GOP clearly hoped to exploit the growing dissatisfaction with U.S. policy in the Far East. Sounding the angry theme of the upcoming campaign, the Republican leader of the Senate charged that Truman's Secretary of State, Dean Acheson, was stained with "the blood of our boys in Korea."

As usual, Senator Joseph McCarthy outdid his colleagues in the bitterness of his attacks on the administration. Within a week after U.S. troops entered the Korean War, McCarthy warned that the crusade against Communism in Asia should not blind Americans to the greater threat of domestic Communists. "Highly placed Red counselors in the State Department are far more deadly than Red machine-gunners at Suwon [in South Korea]," he exclaimed. "It is time to serve notice upon the Communists, fellow travelers, and dupes that they are not going to be able to hide and protect themselves behind a war which would not have been necessary except for their acts." In short, "Communists, dupes and fellow-travelers" in the federal government "plotted the Communist victory in Asia," according to McCarthy. "On their hands and on the hands of the men they have shielded is the blood of American youth."

McCarthy took this message of treachery to over a dozen states during the 1950 election campaign. The Senator received more invitations to speak on behalf of fellow Republicans than all other senators combined. In speech after speech, he called on Americans to vote against "Commiecrats" (Democrats?), who were "prisoners of a bureaucratic Communistic Frankenstein." McCarthy was not alone in making such statements; he was merely the most outrageous.

McCarthy singled out three of his Senate opponents for defeat in 1950: Democratic Majority Leader Scott Lucas of Illinois and two former members of the Tydings Committee—Brien McMahon and Senator Millard Tydings himself. Explaining his feud against these three Democrats who were up for reelection, McCarthy accused them of participating in a cover-up to protect Communists in the government. "Lucas provided the whitewash when I charged there were Communists in high places. McMahon brought the bucket; Tydings the brush."

Much to McCarthy's delight, Lucas and Tydings went down to defeat. Overlooking McMahon's victory, McCarthy claimed credit for ousting Lucas and Tydings from the Senate. In retrospect, other factors—such as Democratic

Party splits in Tydings' state, Maryland—appear to have played a greater role than McCarthy's intervention, but people at the time believed that the Wisconsin Senator had been responsible. Certainly he had been active, especially in the campaign against Tydings. In addition to delivering three speeches on behalf of Tydings' opponent, John Marshall Butler, McCarthy helped raise money for Butler and put his office staff at Butler's disposal. When Butler's election victory followed, observers attributed the result to Joe McCarthy. This belief greatly increased McCarthy's power. His Senate colleagues worried that open opposition to McCarthy would jeopardize their own political careers. After the November elections, *The New York Times* found among Senate Democrats "a general expression of fear that what had happened to Mr. Tydings, with all his standing in the Senate, could happen to any other man in the Senate."

Joe McCarthy also benefited from the growing momentum of the anti-Communist crusade. In September 1950, Congress had passed the Internal Security Act over President Truman's veto. This sweeping law required all so-called "Communist-front organizations" to register with the government, excluded Communists from defense plants, and made it illegal to conspire to commit any act that would "substantially contribute" to the establishment of a dictatorship in the United States. The 1950 law also created the Subversive Activities Control Board and provided for the internment of "subversives" in time of national emergency. Truman blasted the Internal Security Bill as "a mockery of the Bill of Rights," but only seven Senate Democrats had the courage to vote against it. Speaking for the vast majority of Democrats who accepted the law, one senator remarked, "The American people are anxious to have an anti-Communist bill placed on the statute books."

McCarthyism simply represented an extreme form of this hysterical fear of Communism in America. Defining McCarthyism as "getting tough with subversives in Government and outside, and with those who for any reason seek to protect them," the junior Senator from Wisconsin picked up plenty of support around the country. Indeed, most of his admirers had worried about Communists much longer than McCarthy had. Although a formal movement or single organization never attached to McCarthy, he became the symbol of anti-Communism for a wide variety of conservatives who championed right-wing causes and opposed radicals on the political left. McCarthy's most effective support came from right-wing reporters who supplied the Senator with much of his information and then gave prominent coverage to his "revelations" about alleged Communists in government. Willard Edwards, a correspondent for the Chicago *Tribune*, furnished the material for McCarthy's first speech in Wheeling, West Virginia, and then the *Tribune* reported the speech—the only major daily to do so. The extremely conservative publisher of the *Tribune*, Robert R. McCormick, also owned the Washington *Times-Herald*, which aided McCarthy in similar ways. Another right-wing press lord, William Randolph Hearst, Jr., used his string of newspapers to give favorable publicity to McCarthy. Furthermore, Hearst columnists, including Westbrook Pegler and Fulton Lewis, Jr., worked closely with the Senator. Lewis once equated McCarthyism with "Americanism."

Right-wing intellectuals also were attracted to McCarthy. William F. Buckley, Jr., co-authored a 1954 defense of the Senator entitled *McCarthy and His Enemies*. "McCarthyism," the book warmly concluded, "is a weapon in the American arsenal. . . . It is a movement around which men of good will and stern morality can close hands." (Like most other early McCarthy supporters, Buckley has remained to this day a defender of the Senator.)

McCarthy's attacks on "atheistic Communism" picked up some strong support for religious reasons. Like most Americans, McCarthy's fellow Catholics divided sharply in their opinions of the Senator, but he won a significant following among conservative Catholics who were outspoken anti-Communists. This included influential politicians and businessmen such as Joseph Kennedy, the father of John, Robert and Edward (Ted) Kennedy. In addition to providing the Wisconsin Senator with money, the senior Kennedy counted McCarthy as a friend. "I liked Joe McCarthy," he later told an interviewer. "I would see him when I went down to Washington, and when he was visiting in Palm Beach he'd come around to my house for a drink. I invited him to Cape Cod."

McCarthy also found some allies among the hierarchy of the Catholic Church. The best known was Francis Joseph Cardinal Spellman, the archbishop of New York. Asked what he thought about the Senator, Spellman replied in 1953, "He is making America aware of the dangers of Communism."

McCarthy's style of anti-Communism also won support from Protestant fundamentalists. Right-wing ministers, such as Carl McIntyre and Billy James Hargis of the Christian Crusade, sang the Senator's praises. The Reverend Dr. Daniel A. Poling, head of the All American Council to Combat Communism, called McCarthy "a symbol of dynamic defense."

Finally, McCarthy drew into his following "the zanies and zombies and compulsive haters," as author Richard Rovere referred to them in his study *Senator Joe McCarthy*. These were the extreme right-wingers who formed groups with names like the Minute Women of the U.S.A. and the

Alert Council of America. Although their numbers and influence were small, these hard-bitten anti-Communists helped fill the seats at McCarthy rallies.

Above all, of course, McCarthy found a natural following among Republicans. Both GOP leaders and rank-and-file members argued that Democrats were soft on Communism, and they hoped that the issue of Communists in government would help return the Republican Party to power in Washington.

Joe McCarthy never sought to mold his followers into a single organization. Indeed, he showed no signs of seeking political power, much less the presidency. He never even formulated a program. Most observers agree that McCarthy's sole goal was publicity and the attention it brought him. "What he lusted for was glory," Richard Rovere pointed out. "For publicity, he had a talent unmatched by any other politician of this century," Rovere concluded in 1959. More recently, historian Robert Griffith noted about McCarthy, "Publicity and notoriety were both his means and his ends." Another historian, Richard Fried, has argued persuasively that McCarthy built his power in large part on "his genius for publicity, for obtaining maximum mileage from the flimsiest piece of news."

When the new session of Congress met in 1951, Joe McCarthy was riding high. In addition to his growing popularity, he had appeared to demonstrate remarkable influence in the 1950 elections. Although continued Democratic control of the Senate left Republicans like McCarthy without any positions as committee chairmen, the Wisconsin Senator still used the floor of the Senate as an effective forum. Words, after all, were the most important (some said only) weapon in the arsenal of McCarthyism. The Senator continued to outdo himself in his choice of targets that guaranteed him newspaper headlines.

In June 1951, McCarthy unleashed a 60,000-word barrage against General George C. Marshall. The retired general had served as the Army's chief of staff during World War II. In Truman's administration Marshall had held the posts of secretary of state and, since 1950, secretary of defense. As secretary of state in 1947, he had proposed the famous Marshall Plan, a huge American-aid program that was designed to strengthen the economies of European countries and thereby help them resist Communism.

Despite his strong support for the policy of preventing Soviet expansion, Marshall had opened himself to attack from the far right when he supported Truman's decision to fire General Douglas MacArthur for opposing U.S. policy in Korea. McCarthy insisted that the 1951 recall of MacArthur was another blow to America's fortunes in the Cold War. In his long-winded denunciation of Marshall, the Wisconsin Senator asked, "How can we account for our present situation unless we believe that men high in this Government are concerting to deliver us to disaster? This must be the product of a great conspiracy, a conspiracy on a scale so immense as to dwarf any previous such venture in the history of man." McCarthy went on to place General Marshall at the center of this alleged conspiracy to deliver the world to Communism. Without directly saying so, the Senator left the impression that Marshall was a traitor. In defending this famous speech, McCarthy later commented that Marshall "would sell his grandmother for any advantage."

General Marshall did not dignify these charges with a response. Already anxious to leave government service (in part for reasons of health), he resigned as secretary of defense several months later. The vicious attack on Marshall, whom Truman had once described as "the greatest living American," proved that no one was safe from McCarthyism.

In addition to firing salvos at members of the executive branch, McCarthy tried to block the appointments of several people he considered disloyal. With the help of his supporters he sought to deny Anna Rosenberg, a New York businesswoman, confirmation as assistant secretary of defense. The charge that Rosenberg was a Communist blew up in McCarthy's face when his star witness was proven wrong. Nevertheless, the Wisconsin Senator got his headlines, and he moved on seemingly undamaged even though Anna Rosenberg's appointment was approved by the Senate.

In 1951, McCarthy could take some pleasure in the successful campaign to block Senate confirmation of Ambassador Philip C. Jessup as a delegate to the United Nations. McCarthy had earlier charged Jessup with being associated with Communist-front organizations. Although the Tydings Committee had found no basis to question Jessup's loyalty, McCarthy resurrected this charge in 1951, and with the aid of several other senators he successfully prevented Senate approval of the UN appointment. Key senators failed to support Jessup, not because he was disloyal, but because he was "controversial." This showed how guilt by accusation could affect a person's career.

Behind the scenes, McCarthyism claimed other victims. Under pressure from McCarthyites, the Truman administration in 1951 adopted a test of loyalty that shifted the burden of proof to government employees. Originally the Loyalty Review Board had recommended dismissal whenever it found "reasonable grounds for belief that the person is disloyal." Four years later President Truman ordered that anyone be fired if "reasonable doubt" of his or her loyalty existed. In effect, this required that suspected government employees prove they were not disloyal. Since even the most loyal citizens often had difficulty meeting this test, employees previously investigated and cleared now found themselves placed under the cloud of "reasonable doubt." Dismissals and resignations soon followed, especially on the part of the State Department's China experts, who were hounded by McCarthyites. Men like John Stewart Service and John Carter Vincent were declared "loyalty risks" and fired from the department although there had been no previous finding of "reasonable grounds" for doubting their loyalty. Six years later, the Supreme Court ruled that Service had been improperly dismissed, but it was too late. He, like the others, had lost his career and his reputation.

McCarthy's antics did not go completely unchallenged in the Senate. In February 1951 several Democrats jokingly marked the first anniversary of the Wheeling speech. One senator noted that despite "a river of words" McCarthy had not found a single Communist, let alone seven, or fifty-seven, or 205. All that the Wisconsin Senator had done, according to Herbert H. Lehman of New York, was ruin the reputations of "patriotic and loyal Americans."

The strongest voice raised against McCarthy was that of Senator William Benton, a Connecticut Democrat. A newcomer to the Senate, Benton had originally built his reputation in advertising. During the years 1945 to 1947 he had served as an assistant secretary of state, and as a senator he had defended the State Department against McCarthy's attacks. He once denounced the Wisconsin Senator as a "hit-and-run propagandist on the Kremlin model." In August 1951 Benton surprised his Senate colleagues by introducing a resolution calling for an investigation to determine "whether or not [the Rules Committee] should initiate action with a view toward the expulsion from the United States Senate of . . . Joseph R. McCarthy." Benton had little hope of getting the necessary two-thirds Senate vote to expel McCarthy, but he wanted to put the Wisconsin Senator on the spot for a change. Such action might encourage Wisconsin voters to end his career in the 1952 election.

Responding to the resolution in typical fashion, McCarthy called Benton a "mental midget" who had "established himself as a hero of every Communist and crook in and out of government."

The immediate cause of Benton's action was a Senate report on the 1950 senatorial election in Maryland. Senate hearings showed that McCarthy and other "outsiders" had run a vicious "back street" campaign against Millard Tydings, but investigating senators avoided recommending any action against McCarthy. This led Benton to request a more sweeping probe.

In September 1951 Benton was given a chance to defend his call for an investigation of McCarthy. In a public session, Benton presented ten charges to show that the Wisconsin Senator was unfit to hold office. The evidence, ranging from the attack on George Marshall to questionable payments received by McCarthy, was designed to establish that the Wisconsin Senator had "lied" and "practiced deception." After hearing Benton's list of charges, the Privileges and Elections Subcommittee ordered its staff to investigate further.

McCarthy, however, refused to answer the charges. When invited by the subcommittee chairman to respond, McCarthy declared, "Frankly, I . . . do not intend to even read, much less answer, Benton's smear attack." The Wisconsin Senator chose instead to attack the subcommittee and its members. For instance, he accused the group of "stealing" from the taxpayers in order to "aid Benton in his smear attack upon McCarthy." (The Senator often referred to himself by name like this.)

Prodded by McCarthy's blasts, the Subcommittee on Privileges and Elections finally decided to hold formal hearings in May 1952. However, after looking into only one of Benton's ten charges, the panel again stalled. The subcommittee, Benton noted, "cannot be accused of overriding enthusiasm."

Meanwhile, McCarthy continued to put Benton on the defensive. Accusing his opponent of hiding behind senatorial immunity, McCarthy dared Benton to open himself to a libel suit. Benton accepted the challenge, and McCarthy immediately filed a $2 million libel suit. Although McCarthy later dropped the case before it could come to trial in federal court, it had the desired effect. "McCarthy has very cleverly and skillfully tried to work this around so I am on trial, with him as the prosecuting attorney," Benton observed.

The investigation of the Subcommittee on Privileges and Elections came to a formal end in January 1953, when the panel issued its final report. Focusing almost entirely on McCarthy's questionable financial dealings, the report made no recommendations, concluding that "the record should speak for itself." The report took special note of the fact that throughout the inquiry the Wisconsin Senator had shown "a disdain and contempt for the rules and wishes of the entire Senate body." Nevertheless, according to the subcommittee chairman, McCarthy's opponents did not have the votes to move against him.

By 1953, McCarthy had been safely reelected, and in his words the 1952 election showed that "your boss and mine—the American people—do not approve of treason and incompetence and feel that it must be exposed." McCarthy was still riding high.

7 | K_1C_2—A Formula for Victory

Republicans had looked forward to the 1952 elections. Dissatisfaction among voters was so great that it promised to end twenty years of uninterrupted Democratic control of the White House and almost unbroken command of Congress. As the Truman administration limped into its final year, the country was still bogged down in the Korean War, and popular frustration with U.S. foreign policy continued to feed the belief that Communists in government were the cause of setbacks overseas. Furthermore, evidence of corrupt dealings by some Truman appointees undermined public confidence in the administration.

Aware that Americans often voted *against* certain candidates rather than *for* others, Republicans moved to exploit the weaknesses of the Democratic Party in 1952. GOP leaders repeatedly called attention to "Korea, Communism and Corruption." Shortened to K_1C_2, this slogan became a formula for victory in 1952.

Since Joe McCarthy's name was identified with the issue of Communism in government, the Wisconsin Senator could be expected to play a major role in the campaign against Democrats. McCarthy was also up for reelection, which guaranteed him a platform and some newspaper coverage. However, by 1952 so many politicians painted their opponents with the red brush of Communism that McCarthy had to compete for headlines. This, of course, tended to make the publicity-hungry Senator even more reckless.

Despite the fact that he was only a first-term senator, McCarthy had made himself appear so powerful that Republicans in search of the presidential nomination could not afford to overlook him. The Wisconsin Senator was also the darling of the GOP right wing, a group that presidential hopefuls did not want to anger. The positions taken by Senator Robert A. Taft of Ohio showed the kind of balancing act this sometimes required. Although a conservative himself, Taft had questioned McCarthy's "extreme attack" on General George Marshall in 1951, and Taft had remarked in a clear reference to McCarthyism, "I don't think one who overstates his case helps his own case." However, in early 1952 the presidential sweepstakes led Taft to say that McCarthy's campaign against Communists in the State Department was "a great service to the American people."

General Dwight David Eisenhower moved with greater caution. "Ike" had just entered politics after a military career that saw him head Allied troops in Europe during World War II and, most recently, command forces of the North Atlantic Treaty Organization (NATO). He sought the image of a moderate in all things. On the one hand, he spoke of the need to root out "any kind of communistic, subversive or pinkish influence" in government. On the other hand, Ike thought the housecleaning could be done "without besmirching the reputation of any innocent man, or condemning by loose association." Thus, Eisenhower raised the issue of Communism but backed away from that of McCarthyism.

GOP leaders, however, continued to see Joe McCarthy as one of their major weapons against Democrats. At the Republican national convention in July 1952 the Wisconsin Senator was a featured speaker. Millions of voters watching the first nationally televised convention witnessed a strong show of support for Tail Gunner Joe. "When they tell you Joe McCarthy has smeared the names of innocent men, ask them to name just one," proclaimed the temporary chairman who introduced the Wisconsin Senator. "We will not 'turn our backs' at any time on that fighting Marine, the Honorable Joe McCarthy." In the rousing four-minute demonstration that followed, delegates paraded around the convention floor with placards shaped like red herrings and bearing the names "Acheson," "Hiss" and "Lattimore."

McCarthy then delivered the kind of shouting, sarcastic speech his supporters loved. Declaring, "A rough fight is the only fight that Communists understand," the Senator defended his blunt tactics. "We can't fight Communists in the Acheson-Lattimore fashion of hitting them with a perfumed silk handkerchief at the front door while they batter our friends with brass knuckles at the back door."

Determined to pick up the widest possible support, Republicans went on to nominate the war hero Eisenhower for President. Although Ike had criticized McCarthyism in the past, he made it clear in his selection of Senator Richard M. Nixon as his running mate that the campaign would not overlook the issue of Communism in government. Nixon's political reputation was built on his

75

pursuit of Alger Hiss and his slashing attacks on "Reds" and their "pink" sympathizers in government.

After the Republican convention McCarthy was temporarily removed from the political scene by his health. Following major surgery to repair a ruptured diaphragm, he spent over a month recuperating. He reemerged in September to devote a week to his primary campaign in Wisconsin. Against only weak opposition he easily won a lopsided victory in the Republican primary. McCarthy's strong showing added to his image as a political force to reckon with.

This troubled Eisenhower's campaign aides, since the general had tried to keep McCarthy at arm's length. In an August press conference Ike had pledged to work for all Republican candidates, but he refused to give "blanket support to anyone who holds views . . . that would violate my conception of what is decent, right, just and fair." Eisenhower also defended George Marshall, his old friend and former superior. Clearly disputing McCarthy's characterization, Ike called Marshall "a perfect example of patriotism and a loyal servant of the United States."

Eisenhower tried unsuccessfully to avoid any direct contact with the upstart Marine. After telling his staff to omit Wisconsin from his campaign schedule, Ike discovered that his "whistle-stop" tour would pass through Wisconsin. The general decided to use the opportunity to make clear his differences with McCarthy. Upon entering the Badger State, Eisenhower had a strained interview with McCarthy. "I'm going to say that I disagree with you," Ike told the Senator. "If you say that, you'll be booed," McCarthy responded. At the first stop in Green Bay, Eisenhower endorsed the entire Republican ticket as McCarthy, standing nearby, smiled nervously. However, Eisenhower went on to say that his "differences" with the

Senator were "well known." According to Ike, the two men disagreed not over the goal of "ridding the government of ... the subversive and disloyal," but over "method." The general declared that he favored "the right of trial by jury and the principle that people are innocent until proven guilty." At this, McCarthy shook his head, showing strong disagreement.

The climax of the trying day came in Milwaukee that evening. Eisenhower had planned to include in his address a paragraph defending George Marshall as a man "dedicated with singular selflessness and the profoundest patriotism to the service of America." When Wisconsin Republican leaders learned of this, they pressured Eisenhower to cut the reference to Marshall because, they argued, such an open rebuke of McCarthy might cost the election. The presidential candidate agreed to omit the offending paragraph in praise of Marshall. "I handled that subject pretty thoroughly in Denver two weeks ago," he observed, "and there's no reason to repeat it tonight." The speech Ike delivered in Milwaukee smoothed over any differences he might have had with McCarthy. At the conclusion of his talk, Eisenhower even shook McCarthy's hand. "He has met the enemy, and he is theirs," one newspaper commented as Eisenhower left Wisconsin.

Nothing Eisenhower said after that could erase the impression left by the swing through Wisconsin. For the sake of party unity and to assure victory, even Eisenhower would back down when confronted with the power of Joe McCarthy. After his humiliating trip through Wisconsin, Eisenhower went on to praise Marshall and to attack "witch-hunts" and "character assassination." However, the issue of Communists in government remained very much alive.

The redbaiting of the Republicans' national campaign

was left largely in the experienced hands of vice-presidential candidate Richard Nixon. Ike's running mate did not let the voters forget that Adlai Stevenson, the Democratic candidate for President, had once sworn to Alger Hiss's good character. "Somebody had to testify for Alger Hiss," Nixon observed, "but you don't have to elect him President of the United States." Nixon also claimed that Stevenson had "ridiculed and poohpoohed the Communist threat from within." Comparing Eisenhower and Stevenson, Nixon said he would rather have a "khaki-clad President than one clothed in State Department pinks." In case anyone had any doubt where Nixon stood, he went to Wisconsin and endorsed his "good friend, Joe McCarthy."

The Wisconsin Senator played an active, though limited, role in the campaign. In addition to working for his own reelection, he traveled to thirteen other states, largely on behalf of Republican candidates for the Senate. Competing for headlines, McCarthy typically resorted to outrageous statements to generate publicity. "If you'll give me a slippery elm club and put me aboard Adlai Stevenson's campaign train," he declared on one occasion, "I could use it on some of his advisors and I might be able to make a good American out of him."

McCarthy delivered his most famous speech of the campaign in a nationally televised attack on Stevenson. He focused on what he called Stevenson's "aid to the Communist cause." The Senator claimed that the Democratic candidate was "part and parcel of the Acheson-Hiss-Lattimore group," and, to reinforce the link to Hiss, he intentionally referred to "Alger—I mean Adlai." What followed was a string of untruths and half-truths that McCarthy tried to pass off as "cold-documented history" by holding up newspaper clippings and photographs. Directing his comments to "the millions of loyal Democrats who no longer have a party in Washington," McCarthy engaged in the kind of guilt by accusation that could have convinced only those who had already decided to vote for Eisenhower.

The outcome of the 1952 election should have raised some questions about McCarthy's alleged power. Although Eisenhower won, the Communist issue was not the only issue in the campaign, and McCarthy was not the only one to use it. Korea and corruption proved the most potent part of the Republican formula, K_1C_2. Furthermore, McCarthy was reelected senator, but he ran well behind Eisenhower in Wisconsin. In fact, McCarthy got the fewest votes of any Republican on the state ticket. In other states, a number of senatorial candidates endorsed by McCarthy had won, but several who had his stamp of approval had gone down to defeat. Even the victories of candidates backed by McCarthy were often the result of other factors. Indeed, Eisenhower's drawing power was much more influential than McCarthy's intervention. This was especially true in Connecticut, where McCarthy's outspoken opponent, William Benton, was defeated. Although McCarthy made three trips to Connecticut to campaign against Benton, the Democratic Senator got more votes than Stevenson, and his defeat was a result of the Eisenhower landslide. Nevertheless, McCarthy pointed with great joy at the Connecticut election, asking a reporter, "How do you like what happened to my friend Benton?"

One study of the 1952 election concluded that McCarthy's aid may have actually hurt the candidates he backed. Political analyst Louis H. Bean found that candidates endorsed by McCarthy ran an average of 5 percent behind other Republicans.

Despite this evidence of Joe McCarthy's weakness, the

legend of his political power continued to grow. Friend and foe alike exaggerated the influence of both the Wisconsin Senator and the issue of Communism. Right-wing columnist Westbrook Pegler called McCarthy "one of the most popular Republicans in the country, with his own bandwagon capable of cruising far beyond the borders of his own Wisconsin." A liberal Democrat, Senator Hubert H. Humphrey, commented privately after the 1952 election, "There is no doubt that Senator McCarthy's power lies with his hold on public opinion. The fate of ex-Senators Tydings and Benton would indicate that opposing Senator McCarthy within the Senate—as a political matter—is not likely to succeed."

This illusion of power did in fact make McCarthy powerful. As long as politicians, especially U.S. senators, feared the wrath of McCarthy, he would steamroll ahead.

Judge McCarthy on the bench
in July 1942.

McCarthy debriefing marines
following bombing missions in
the Pacific.

"Tail Gunner Joe."

McCarthy addressing
Republican women's clubs in
October 1950 on behalf of
senatorial candidate Everett
Dirksen.

Republican Presidential candidate Dwight D. Eisenhower and Joe McCarthy shake hands following Eisenhower's campaign speech in Milwaukee, October 1952.

McCarthy with his wife Jean in
October 1953.

Senator McCarthy emerges
from an inspection of the radar
lab at Fort Monmouth, New
Jersey, after probing for
security leaks in the Signal
Corps. At far right is Secretary
of the Army Robert Stevens.

McCarthy as he appeared before millions of Americans on TV
during the Army-McCarthy hearings.

McCarthy (center) confers with Senator Stuart Symington (left) and committee minority counsel Robert Kennedy (right), March 1954.

McCarthy, during hearings, holding original "undoctored" photo of Stevens, Schine, and third man. Senator Henry Jackson sits at left; Robert Kennedy is at far left in the back.

McCarthy and G. David Schine put on a four-handed greeting when Schine arrives for the Army-McCarthy hearings in Washington, in April 1954.

McCarthy and Cohn tête-à-tête during a recess of the Senate Investigations subcommittee.

McCarthy being sworn in as a witness at the Army-McCarthy hearings. Welch sits at McCarthy's left, with Stevens directly behind. May 5, 1954.

Army Counsel Joseph Welch
(far left) exchanges views with
McCarthy during the hearings.

McCarthy replying to Senator
Ralph Flanders' (standing)
declaration that he would take
the Senate floor a third time to
attack McCarthy. Roy Cohn is
at center.

McCarthy in January 1957, just a few months before his death.

8 | The Grand Inquisitor

The issue of Communism in government had proved
a useful political weapon for Republicans. Although
Joe McCarthy had not turned up a single Communist,
the GOP had successfully exploited his accusations to
undermine confidence in the Truman Administration.
Along with the issues of Korea and corruption, the charge
of "twenty years of treason" helped give Republicans
control of both the White House and Congress in 1953.
With the GOP in power, McCarthy would become more
of a liability than a help if he continued to charge that
Communists were tolerated in the government service.
The question remained whether the Wisconsin Senator
understood that. If not, could the Republican Party keep
the publicity-hungry Senator under control?

Once returned to power, Republicans showed that they
did not trust McCarthy. Party leaders refused to give him
the chairmanship of a powerful Senate committee.

Another McCarthyite, William Jenner of Indiana, was made chairman of the Senate's Internal Security Committee, which could be expected to handle any investigation of subversives. McCarthy was sidetracked to a minor post, chairman of the Government Operations Committee, which had charge of a variety of tasks, including the assignment of office space. Obviously pleased with this coup, Senate Republican leader Robert Taft bragged to writer Richard Rovere, "We've got McCarthy where he can't do any harm."

Republicans like Taft overlooked the fact that McCarthy had originally become prominent without any committee chairmanship at all. Even a relatively insignificant Senate committee could be used to build the power of an aggressive chairman. The head of a Senate committee had the authority to appoint subcommittee members, select staff members, choose what issues to pursue, call hearings and summon witnesses. Needless to say, Joe McCarthy took full advantage of these powers and stretched them to their limit. The Committee on Government Operations had a Permanent Investigations Subcommittee which had sweeping authority to look into government operations at all levels. McCarthy chaired the subcommittee, and he appointed sympathetic Republican senators to join him. For chief counsel he selected Roy M. Cohn, a bright young lawyer from New York who had helped prosecute internal-security cases.

Even before taking these actions, McCarthy had clearly stated that he had no intention of giving up the issue that had made him famous. "We have complete jurisdiction of the anti-Communist fight," he told an interviewer. "I'm not retiring from the field of exposing Communists."

McCarthy lost no time launching his career as grand inquisitor in search of Communists in government. His first target was the Voice of America, an arm of the State Department that was designed to broadcast the American point of view to some eighty foreign countries. With radio programs in over forty different languages, the Voice of America was considered an important weapon in the ideological Cold War with Russia. In February 1953, three years after his first speech in Wheeling, Senator McCarthy announced that his subcommittee would investigate a plot to sabotage propaganda broadcasts by the Voice of America. This explosive charge made headline news across the country.

Typically, McCarthy's investigations produced much less than promised, but his sensational charges damaged the Voice of America and a number of people connected with it. The hearings by McCarthy's subcommittee featured discontented Voice employees who aired a variety of complaints. Several said that anti-Communist material had been cut from their broadcasts. Another claimed to have lost her job after she gave a favorable review to the autobiography of Whittaker Chambers.

For McCarthy, the ultimate proof of subversion in the Voice of America came in testimony about the disputed location of two radio transmitters. In an effort to avoid atmospheric interference, the Voice had begun construction of two radio towers, one in North Carolina and the other near Seattle, Washington. Code-named Baker East and Baker West, the sites had been selected after extensive electronic studies by outside experts, including scientists at the Massachusetts Institute of Technology. However, McCarthy found a discontented Voice engineer who had opposed these locations, and he used this testimony in an attempt to prove that mismanagement and sabotage had destroyed the effectiveness of America's anti-Communist propaganda. By refusing to call any other experts and by carefully leading his star witness, McCarthy created the impression he wanted. "Now, has it ever been *suggested*," McCarthy asked, "by those who have worked with you in the Voice that this mislocation of stations . . . has not been entirely as the result of incompetence, but that some of it *may* have been purposely planned that way?" When the friendly witness answered positively, the Senator had all the proof of sabotage he needed.

Once again many newspaper readers undoubtedly overlooked McCarthy's failure to locate real evidence of sabotage. Indeed, millions of Americans no longer needed any newspaper reports about McCarthy, because these hearings were televised. Seeing McCarthy in action probably increased his following among people who did not understand that he deliberately used distortion and innuendo to create false impressions.

The Voice of America investigation once again showed the harm caused by McCarthyism. Because of the suspicions raised by the Senator, the State Department dumped the Baker project to build the world's two most powerful radio transmitters. One reporter called this "a mighty victory for the Kremlin." Even more disturbing was the suicide of a Voice engineer who had worked on the project. He left a note saying, "You see, once the dogs are set upon you, everything you have done from the beginning of time is suspect." McCarthy quickly announced he had no evidence of any wrongdoing on the part of the dead engineer.

Having mined all the publicity he could out of the Voice of America, McCarthy moved on to the International Information Agency (IIA), which ran two hundred overseas libraries for the State Department. These libraries in sixty-five countries housed over two million books by American authors. Directed at foreign readers, the libraries were considered another tool in America's ideological battle with the Soviet Union. Senator McCarthy captured headlines when he charged that the IIA libraries contained thirty thousand books by authors whose loyalty was suspect. The list of 418 writers included a few Communists, but most of those targeted by McCarthy were either left-wingers or anti-Communist liberals. Reading like a who's who in American letters, the list of suspect authors included the names of Sherwood Anderson, W. H. Auden, Theodore Dreiser and Edna Ferber. One of those on the list was Foster Rhea Dulles, an anti-Communist historian and cousin of the Secretary of State, John Foster Dulles. Seeing the name, the Secretary of State wondered aloud, "Why have they got my cousin on that list?"

The ridiculous idea of banning books in the name of freedom did not prevent a fearful administration from caving in. Secretary of State Dulles fired off an order that declared, "No material by any Communists, fellow travelers, et cetera, will be used under any circumstances by any IIA media." The definition of "et cetera" was apparently left open to interpretation, but it showed how far McCarthyism could go. The State Department went on to draw up a list of offending books that it ordered withdrawn from overseas libraries. Getting into the spirit of things, several overzealous employees actually burned copies of the forbidden books. Secretary of State Dulles immediately called a halt to book burning. McCarthy, however, implied approval of burning books when he once asked, "What would you do, pay for storing them?"

The search for mismanagement and subversion in the International Information Agency took two of McCarthy's aides on a whirlwind tour of Europe. Chief counsel Roy Cohn was accompanied by G. David Schine, an unpaid committee consultant who would become a leading figure in the McCarthy drama. Cohn and Schine were a curious contrast. Both were twenty-six years old, but the similarity stopped there. Cohn, short and dark-complected, had bulging eyes which gave him a menacing look. Schine was tall and good-looking. While Cohn had become known as a brilliant lawyer in his prosecution of internal-security cases, his friend Schine, the son of a rich businessman, had a reputation as a playboy. Schine had established himself as an expert on Communism by writing a six-page pamphlet, entitled "Definition of Communism," which he distributed through his father's hotel chain. Although the pamphlet was filled with errors, it came to Cohn's attention, and he encouraged McCarthy to take on Schine as a committee consultant. Some cynics suggested that the Senator was more interested in the young man's money and his access to resort hotels.

The unlikely team of Cohn and Schine first captured headlines on their European tour of April 1953. Followed by a herd of journalists, the pair seemed unsure of their mission. However, like their boss, they seemed chiefly interested in publicity. Hopping from city to city, they met in private with U.S. diplomats, talked with former Communists and dined with foreign officials. In one typical performance, Cohn and Schine visited the Russian Information Center in Vienna. A check of the Soviet library turned up books by Theodore Dreiser and Mark Twain, both of whom were dead. With reporters in tow, Cohn and Schine then rushed to the nearby U.S. Information Center and made much of the fact that the American library also contained works by authors like Dreiser and Twain that had been found acceptable by the Soviets. Exactly what this proved was never made clear.

After the return of Cohn and Schine, McCarthy used the book issue to haul suspect writers before his committee. In televised hearings, he browbeat witnesses, none of whom was a government employee or even accused of any illegal act. Some writers tried to protect themselves by publicly admitting that their previous leftist ideas had been wrong. Others simply refused to answer questions about Communist affiliations, and they pointed out that under the Fifth Amendment to the Constitution the committee could not force anyone to testify against himself.

McCarthy also used these hearings to go after James A. Wechsler, editor of the New York *Post*. Wechsler had long admitted that he had once belonged to the Young Communist League while a student in the 1930s. Although an outspoken opponent of Communism by the time McCarthy caught up with him, Wechsler found himself under the gun supposedly because he had written a book discovered in an IIA library. However, it quickly became clear that the Senator's real purpose was to harass the editor for his newspaper's attacks on McCarthyism. Wechsler survived the grilling, but he warned that he was probably "the first in a long line of editors who are going to be called ... because they refuse to equate 'McCarthyism' with patriotism."

The book controversy finally stirred President Eisenhower to a rare expression of concern. In off-the-cuff remarks during a commencement address in June, he advised Dartmouth College graduates, "Don't join the book burners.... Don't be afraid to go into your library and read every book." Asked later if he was referring to McCarthy, the President backed away with the statement "I think we will get along faster if we remember that I do not talk personalities." Eisenhower told aides that he shied away from a confrontation with McCarthy because "nothing would probably please [McCarthy] more than to get the publicity that would be generated by public repudiation by the President." In his most famous remark about McCarthy Ike said privately, "I will not get into the gutter with that guy."

While the Republican administration adopted a hands-off policy toward McCarthy, leading Democrats also hesitated to do battle with the Wisconsin Senator. Outnumbered by Republicans in Congress, Democrats saw little to be gained by attacking McCarthy. For one thing, the Wisconsin Senator was still directing most of his blows at the State Department, which was now controlled by Republicans. Democratic leaders saw no reason to divert McCarthy's attention. Senate Minority Leader Lyndon B. Johnson said he refused to enter a debate where Democrats would wind up defending the position "Resolved, that Communism is good for the United States." According to the Democratic national chairman, McCarthy was "the Republicans' responsibility and we have been doing all right in making them bear the burden he is, and thus eventually forcing them to discipline him."

Despite the reluctance of most politicians to take on McCarthy, a few courageous senators spoke out. Herbert H. Lehman, a New York liberal near the end of his long political career, forcefully condemned "creeping McCarthyism," which, he argued, was undermining America's leadership of the free world.

Outside the Senate, anti-McCarthy forces began to organize in 1953. The National Committee for an Effective Congress (NCEC), a liberal group that aided like-minded senators in their campaigns, turned its attention to McCarthyism in early 1953. Convinced that the Wisconsin Senator was the greatest obstacle to an effective Congress, leaders of the NCEC brought together anti-McCarthyites to form the so-called Clearing House, a center that collected information on McCarthy and quietly directed it to his opponents, especially in the Senate. As the Senate opposition to McCarthy grew, so too would the importance of the Clearing House as a fact-finding group to expose McCarthy's weaknesses.

The first opportunity came in June 1953, when McCarthy selected a new staff member for his Investigations Subcommittee. The job of executive director went to J. B. Matthews, a Methodist minister who had had a brief flirtation with the political left in the 1930s but had turned quickly to the far right. As an overnight expert on Communism, Matthews had worked first for the House Un-American Activities Committee and then for the Hearst newspapers. His appointment to the McCarthy committee caused a furor when it was discovered that the current issue of the magazine *American Mercury* contained an outrageous article by Matthews. Entitled "Reds and Our Churches," the article charged: "The largest single group supporting the Communist apparatus in the United States today is composed of Protestant clergymen."

Democrats moved to exploit McCarthy's obvious blunder in appointing a man who would make such a charge. Angered by the slur against Protestant ministers, Senator John McClellan of Arkansas led the Democratic minority on the Investigations Subcommittee in demanding Matthews' dismissal. When McCarthy initially refused, additional pressure came from the White House in the form of a presidential statement denouncing "irresponsible attacks that sweepingly condemn the whole of any group of citizens." With the religious community also up in arms, a Republican on the McCarthy subcommittee, Charles E. Potter of Michigan, joined Democrats in voting to fire Matthews. However, Potter tried to smooth over his defection by supporting a Republican resolution that declared the subcommittee chairman (McCarthy) had full power to hire and fire staff members. Rejecting this interpretation of Senate rules, the three Democrats resigned from the McCarthy subcommittee. This unusual step, coupled with Matthews' firing, marked the first noticeable setback for McCarthy.

True to form, the Senator tried to mask his defeat with a diversion. On July 10, 1953, the same day newspapers announced Matthews' firing, they also carried the sensational news that McCarthy was chasing after Allen Dulles, head of the Central Intelligence Agency (CIA) and brother of Secretary of State John Foster Dulles. The CIA chief found himself under attack because he refused to let CIA employees testify before congressional committees. The Wisconsin Senator expressed particular concern about CIA aide William Bundy, whom McCarthy accused of once contributing to a defense fund for Alger Hiss.

McCarthy's proposed investigation of the CIA produced a sharp rebuke from Senator A. S. "Mike" Monroney, a Democrat from Oklahoma. Monroney argued that a congressional probe of the country's top-secret intelligence agency "would disclose to our enemies information and data that even the Kremlin's best spy apparatus could not get for them." Moreover, Monroney went on, "I question the oft-stated claim that only the Senator from Wisconsin stands between us and internal subversion." Stressing the absurdity of relying on amateurs to root out Communists, Monroney concluded, "I doubt that Messrs. Cohn and Schine, J. B. Matthews, or even the distinguished junior Senator from Wisconsin measure up in ability to the Federal Bureau of Investigation."

The day after Monroney's speech, McCarthy met with Allen Dulles and then announced that he would not investigate the CIA.

Increasingly on the defensive, McCarthy tried to get Democrats to rejoin his subcommittee. He suggested that Democrats didn't "want to take part in uncovering the graft and corruption of the old Truman-Acheson Administration." However, neither insults nor appeals for help brought back boycotting Democrats.

McCarthy did not let the absence of subcommittee Democrats stand in the way of his frantic search for Communists. After Congress adjourned in August, he started a series of one-man investigations. The Wisconsin Senator first turned up evidence of lax security in the Government Printing Office (GPO), the agency responsible for printing government documents, some of which contained secret information. Testimony indicated that a GPO bookbinder, Edward M. Rothschild, might have once been involved in Communist activities. When called to testify in public hearings, Rothschild and his wife stood on their constitutional right to refuse to answer McCarthy's questions. Informed of this, the GPO immediately suspended Rothschild. For McCarthy the discovery of a bookbinder with a questionable background was proof that the government's loyalty boards were not doing their job. "This is the most fantastic picture," McCarthy exclaimed. "For the last three years I've been talking about the complete incompetence of the loyalty boards. Here is an example." However, McCarthy overlooked the fact that the Printing Office was an arm of the Congress, not of the executive branch he had been accusing for so long.

In September 1953, McCarthy strayed so far afield that he raised legal questions about his authority. The episode involved Corliss Lamont, a philosophy professor at Columbia University, who had openly defended the Soviet Union in books and in public meetings. This was perfectly legal, and Lamont was not an example of Communism in government, because, for one thing, he had never held a government job. However, McCarthy discovered that some books purchased by the government contained quotes by the left-wing professor. On this pretext, the Senator subpoenaed Lamont to testify on September 23, 1953.

Since Corliss Lamont was a private citizen, he took the position that his writings and speeches were protected by the Constitution's First Amendment. Nevertheless, Lamont told McCarthy in a secret session, "To dispose of a question causing current apprehension, I am a loyal American and I am not now and never have been a member of the Communist Party." When Lamont refused to answer any other questions about his beliefs, McCarthy asked the Senate to cite the professor for contempt of Congress, which is punishable in the courts. The Senate overwhelmingly agreed, and a prolonged court battle resulted.

Several years later, federal courts ruled that Senator McCarthy had no authority to investigate subversion. The courts pointed out that McCarthy's Committee on Government Operations was empowered to look into "improper influence in government," but that, according to a Senate directive, any inquiries undertaken were *"in no way* [to] interfere or transgress those investigations which other Senate and House of Representatives committees may be engaged in making in comparable areas of government operation, such as *subversion."* (Emphasis added.) Since other Senate and House committees were actively engaged in probing subversion, it was evident that McCarthy had illegally tried to duplicate their efforts. However, at the height of his power, the grand inquisitor had gone largely unchallenged. McCarthy took advantage of his own audacity and the fear of his fellow senators to do whatever he chose.

In the fall of 1953, Joe McCarthy briefly turned his attention from Communists to romance. On September 17 he announced his engagement to Jean Kerr, a research assistant in his office. Two weeks later McCarthy married the former college beauty queen in a Washington ceremony that was a measure of the Senator's standing. Wedding guests included Vice-President and Mrs. Nixon and several Cabinet members. Although President Eisenhower did not attend, his most important assistant, Sherman Adams, did. From the Senate came a number of Republicans and at least one Democrat, Senator John F. Kennedy of Massachusetts, who had recently married Jacqueline Bouvier. In addition to the honored guests, over three thousand people gathered outside St. Matthew's Roman Catholic Cathedral to cheer McCarthy and his bride.

The forty-five-year-old McCarthy had postponed marriage because he did not think it fit with his hectic life. As if to prove that marriage would not change him, he rushed from his wedding to New York City to accept the Bill of Rights Award given annually by the Wall Street Post of the American Legion. A Wall Street crowd of five thousand people heard McCarthy attack "eggheaded elements of the press, radio and politics" and call for "a halt to the cringing, whining, crawling appeasement of the last twenty years." From New York, McCarthy and his bride flew to the Bahamas for a honeymoon. However, their stay was brief.

In early October, McCarthy cut short his honeymoon and returned to Washington with the startling news that he would investigate a breakdown of security at a U.S. Army laboratory. McCarthy had decided to take on the U.S. military in an historic battle that would ultimately last a year and cause the Senator's downfall.

9 | McCarthy Versus the Army

By the end of 1953, Senator Joseph McCarthy had failed for over two years to find a single Communist, much less a spy, employed by the federal government. Most of McCarthy's efforts since his first speech in Wheeling had focused on the State Department. Apparently aware that he had mined that agency for all the publicity he could, the Wisconsin Senator turned to the Department of Defense. Here was a target guaranteed to reap headlines. What could be worse than possible Communist infiltration of the U.S. military?

In October 1953 Senator McCarthy announced that his committee would investigate "extremely dangerous espionage" in the ranks of the U.S. Army. This charge focused on an army installation at Fort Monmouth, New Jersey. There the Signal Corps operated highly secret laboratories that developed radar and other electronic gadgetry. As usual, McCarthy was not the first to raise questions about security at the sensitive research complex. In fact, doubts were brought up during the spy trial of Julius Rosenberg who had worked at Fort Monmouth during World War II. More recently, the House Un-American Activities Committee had probed charges that security at the Signal Corps laboratories had broken down, but the committee reported in 1952 that it had turned up nothing. Although the Signal Corps employees at Fort Monmouth had been repeatedly checked by both Army Intelligence and the FBI, McCarthy seized on the fact that several employees were suspended in the fall of 1953. With Fort Monmouth already associated in the popular mind with intrigue, it made a natural target for McCarthy's style of investigation.

The McCarthy hearings on Fort Monmouth were held in executive session at the Federal Courthouse in New York City. Closed to the press and the public, the hearings were supposedly secret. However, McCarthy periodically emerged and leaked bits and pieces of testimony to reporters. His version was, of course, colored to generate sensational publicity. The resulting newspaper headlines from October tell much of the story: "SPYING IS CHARGED AT FORT MONMOUTH," "ARMY RADAR DATA REPORTED MISSING," "McCARTHY CHARGES SOVIET GOT SECRETS."

Behind the closed doors of the hearing room, McCarthy and his staff badgered witnesses in an effort to break down their stories. The grilling was designed to unhinge the witnesses. The lawyer for a number of Fort Monmouth employees complained that McCarthy's technique "smacks of Star Chamber and the Inquisitions of old, and what you hear about Behind-the-Iron-Curtain countries."

The impact of this process can be seen in one case. On October 17 *The New York Times* reported on page one: "RADAR WITNESS BREAKS DOWN: WILL TELL ALL ABOUT SPY RING."

The news story went on to say that the unnamed witness had broken down and agreed to tell McCarthy's committee all he knew about an espionage ring. "The witness," McCarthy related, "has indicated a great fear of the spy ring which is operating within Government agencies, including the Signal Corps." A month later, the truth about this case was revealed in a *New York Times* article headlined "MYSTERY WITNESS DISPUTES M'CARTHY." It turned out that the witness had in fact broken down and cried under the pressure of cross-examination, but he denied ever saying he knew anything about any spy ring. Asked about this, McCarthy responded, "I would not want to comment."

The fact was that McCarthy never found any Communists or spies operating at Fort Monmouth. Although a number of Signal Corps employees were temporarily suspended and seven were dismissed as "security risks," all were eventually reinstated. As Fred J. Cook concluded in his book *The Nightmare Decade*, "Fort Monmouth, far from producing a flourishing spy ring or a nest of communists, in the end could not even produce a security risk!"

The Fort Monmouth investigation did, however, produce plenty of publicity, which was, after all, what Joe McCarthy really wanted. The probe also inevitably strained relations between McCarthy and the administration. Yet President Eisenhower still tried to avoid an open break with the rampaging Senator. Ike's Secretary of the Army, Robert Stevens, also tried to prevent an open rupture. At the peak of the Signal Corps inquiry, Secretary Stevens toured Fort Monmouth with McCarthy. Standing beside the Senator, Stevens bravely declared, "This is the kind of teamwork between the executive and legislative branches of the government which will clean up any situation which needs cleaning up."

McCarthy refused to let sleeping dogs lie. Although Eisenhower kept silent on McCarthy's probe of the Army, the Wisconsin Senator attacked the President. The blowup came about in a curious way. In November 1953 Attorney General Herbert Brownell charged that in 1946 President Truman had nominated Harry Dexter White to be executive director of the International Monetary Fund despite FBI reports alleging that White was a Soviet agent. Truman denied the charge, and in a televised response he angrily accused the Eisenhower administration of resorting to "McCarthyism." Truman defined McCarthyism as "the corruption of truth, the abandonment of our historical devotion to fair play . . . [and] the use of the big lie and unfounded accusations."

McCarthy immediately demanded equal television time to reply. The networks agreed, but McCarthy devoted little of his allotted time to Truman. "He is of no more importance than any other defeated politician," the Senator remarked. (Truman, of course, had not been defeated in 1952, since he had not even run for reelection.) After taking some potshots at the Democrats, McCarthy turned to the Eisenhower administration. "Let's take a look at the Republican Party," he said. "Unfortunately in some cases our batting average has not been too good." As examples McCarthy pointed to the retention in the State Department of John Paton Davies, Jr. ("part and parcel of the old Acheson-Lattimore-Vincent-White-Hiss group"), the failure to get captured American fliers out of China, and the continued "blood-trade" between American allies and Red China.

Although McCarthy had thrown down the gauntlet, the Eisenhower administration refused to pick it up. Despite the urging of several anti-McCarthy aides, the President still maintained his silence.

Vice-President Nixon served as a go-between trying to prevent a complete break between McCarthy and the Republican administration. While vacationing at a Florida resort in December, Nixon met privately with the Wisconsin Senator. According to Nixon biographer Earl Mazo, the Vice-President advised McCarthy, "Don't pull your punches at all on Communists in government. . . . On the other hand, remember that this is your administration. That the people in this administration, including [Army Secretary] Bob Stevens, are just as dedicated as you are to cleaning out people who are subversive. Give them a chance to do the job." Nixon also suggested that McCarthy should investigate corruption in the old Truman administration. McCarthy seemed to go along with these ideas until press reports made it appear that the Wisconsin Senator had agreed to ease off on the Communist issue. Always the fighter, McCarthy denied he had made any such deal.

As the administration fended off McCarthy's blows, most Democrats enjoyed the spectacle and maintained their silence. Asked about McCarthy, Senate Minority Leader Lyndon B. Johnson declared, "I have nothing to say except that he is a Republican problem."

At the start of 1954, Joe McCarthy was at the peak of his popularity. A January Gallup poll showed 50 percent of those questioned holding a favorable opinion of the Wisconsin Senator. This was up from 34 percent the previous June.

Nevertheless, storm clouds were on the horizon as McCarthy continued his running battle with the U.S. Army. In his search for Communists, the Senator demanded that the Defense Department open its confidential loyalty and security files. Rebuffed by the administration, McCarthy threatened in January 1954 to subpoena the loyalty and security appeals board that had handled the cases of Fort Monmouth scientists. Republican leaders in both the administration and Congress talked McCarthy out of this direct challenge to the President. Nevertheless, the Army–McCarthy feud intensified.

Early in 1954, McCarthy came the closest ever in his search for Communists in government. He discovered that the Army had drafted and given an officer's commission to a New York dentist, Irving Peress, even though Peress had refused to answer questions on army forms about his political beliefs and affiliations. After about a year, the Army turned up this fact and began steps to discharge Peress, who was then stationed at Camp Kilmer, New Jersey. Meanwhile, Peress had been automatically promoted to the rank of major along with thousands of other doctors and dentists, as provided for in the Doctor Draft Law. At that point, McCarthy learned about this case of possible subversion, and he called Peress before his committee. Peress appeared voluntarily at a closed session on January 30, 1954, but he stood on his Fifth Amendment right and refused to answer questions about Communist affiliations that might tend to incriminate him. McCarthy then wrote a letter to the Secretary of the Army demanding that Peress be court-martialed. At the same time, Peress requested an immediate discharge, which the Army granted on February 2, apparently in hopes that that would end the embarrassing case.

However, this gave McCarthy the opening he wanted to put the Army on the defensive. He first called Brigadier General Ralph W. Zwicker, the commander of Camp Kilmer, where Peress had last served. On February 18, at a closed hearing in New York, McCarthy grilled Zwicker in an attempt to find out who had processed Peress' quick discharge request. Zwicker did not appear sufficiently cooperative to McCarthy.

"General, let's try and be truthful," the Senator lectured. "I am going to keep you here as long as you keep hedging and hemming."

Clearly resenting this, Zwicker responded, "I don't like to have anyone impugn my honesty, which you just did."

"Either your honesty or your intelligence," McCarthy shot back.

The Senator later asked Zwicker whether the officer responsible for the Peress discharge would himself be removed from the military. When Zwicker answered in the negative, McCarthy lashed out, "Then, General, you should be removed from any command. Any man who has been given the honor of being promoted to general and who says, 'I will protect another general who protected Communists,' is not fit to wear that uniform, General."

This personal attack on a highly decorated military officer angered Army Secretary Robert Stevens. In a press release on February 21, Stevens announced that he had ordered Zwicker not to reappear as scheduled before the McCarthy committee. "I cannot permit loyal officers of our forces to be subjected to such unwarranted treatment," Stevens declared.

Learning that the Army Secretary would block the general's reappearance, McCarthy privately warned Stevens, "Just go ahead and try it, Robert. I am going to kick the brains out of anyone who protects Communists!"

Reflecting on his questioning of General Zwicker, McCarthy later told one audience, "I was too temperate. If I were doing it today I would be much stronger in my language."

Continuing to act as a go-between in the interest of GOP harmony, Vice-President Nixon tried to defuse the explosive situation. He met with several Republicans on McCarthy's subcommittee and asked them to mediate the dispute between McCarthy and Stevens. The GOP senators did this by carefully arranging Stevens' surrender. At a famous chicken luncheon on Capitol Hill, Stevens accepted a so-called "memorandum of understanding" in which he publicly agreed to give McCarthy the names of all the officers involved in the Peress case and to make them available to testify. Flaunting his victory, McCarthy told a reporter that Stevens could not have surrendered more completely "if he had got down on his knees."

After the humiliating retreat by Stevens, several newspapers called for his resignation. The Secretary tried to save face—and his career—by issuing a statement which bravely declared, "I shall never accede to the abuse of army personnel." He also claimed that he had received assurances that if officers testified before McCarthy they would get proper treatment. McCarthy promptly labeled this "completely false."

As Republicans tried desperately to heal the breach, it steadily widened. At a press conference on March 3, Eisenhower said that the administration would not allow anyone in the executive branch to "submit to any kind of personal humiliation when testifying before congressional committees." The President coupled this mild support for Stevens with a refusal to answer any questions about McCarthy.

Overlooking Eisenhower's persistent attempts to avoid a personal fight, McCarthy held a follow-up press conference. He branded Peress "a sacred cow of certain Army brass." In an obvious reference to Eisenhower's call for "fair play" for committee witnesses, McCarthy exclaimed, "If a stupid, arrogant or witless man in a position of power appears before our committee and is found aiding the Communist Party, he will be exposed."

A week later, a Republican senator, Ralph E. Flanders of Vermont, attacked McCarthy in a Senate speech. Asking what party McCarthy could possibly belong to, Flanders remarked, "One must conclude that his is a one-man party, and that its name is 'McCarthyism.'" Ridiculing McCarthy's efforts to root out Communists, Flanders observed, "He goes forth to battle, and proudly returns with the scalp of a pink Army dentist."

That same evening, millions of Americans watched a nationally televised exposé of McCarthy. The broadcast was a documentary prepared for Edward R. Murrow's weekly program *See It Now.* The film footage showed McCarthy at his worst—browbeating witnesses, contradicting himself, belching and picking his nose. At the end of the telecast Murrow reflected, "We must not confuse dissent with disloyalty. We must always remember that accusation is not proof." Murrow concluded, "This is no time for men who oppose Senator McCarthy's methods to keep silent, or for those who approve." This attack on McCarthy brought a flood of responses from viewers, most of whom supported Murrow.

Two days later, on March 11, the Defense Department dropped a bombshell. In a thirty-four-page report the Army charged that Senator McCarthy and his chief counsel, Roy Cohn, had sought favored treatment for G. David Schine, the subcommittee consultant and Cohn's friend. This latest episode in the continuing saga of McCarthy versus the Army had been developing behind the scenes for months. It had started in the summer of 1953 when Schine had received his draft notice. Both Roy Cohn and Senator McCarthy used their influence in an effort to get Schine a direct commission as an officer. When army brass refused to make the college dropout an officer, Roy Cohn went directly to Army Secretary Stevens and argued that Schine should be assigned to an army post near New York because his work for the McCarthy committee was so important. Throughout the fall, Cohn kept pressing Stevens, but the Army Secretary insisted that Schine would be handled like any other draftee. After his induction in November 1953, Schine was sent to Fort Dix, New Jersey, for basic training. However, he received unusual favors, including frequent passes and release from routine duties. He also spent much of his time on the telephone, supposedly doing work for McCarthy.

The Army's "chronology" of the Schine case listed forty-four separate occasions on which Cohn and McCarthy allegedly applied improper pressure. According to the Army, Cohn had been the most persistent, threatening to "wreck the Army" unless it granted Schine special treatment. The Army turned its chronology of events over to senators on McCarthy's subcommittee, and the press immediately published the explosive story.

McCarthy typically defended himself and Cohn by making outrageous countercharges. The Senator accused the Army of "blackmail," contending that the military had held Schine as a "hostage" to force McCarthy to end his investigation of the Army. The Wisconsin Senator also released documents that quoted Army Secretary Stevens as promising "plenty of dirt" if McCarthy would leave the Army alone and go after the Navy and the Air Force. Stevens labeled this accusation "utterly untrue."

As the charges and countercharges flew wildly, pressure mounted for a formal investigation to get at the truth. At that point, McCarthy's future was riding not on a Communist but on G. David Schine, a playboy turned expert on Communism who had been drafted by the Army.

The Army–McCarthy
10 | Hearings

The upshot of the long-running feud between Senator McCarthy and the Army was a demand for a full-scale investigation. As soon as senators learned on March 11, 1954, of the Army's charges in the case of Private Schine, Democrats called for an inquiry. Republicans resisted, with Senator Everett M. Dirksen of Illinois suggesting privately that the Senate should bury the issue and let "the grass grow over it." Senator John McClellan, a powerful Democrat on McCarthy's subcommittee, argued that the Senate could not "afford to do anything that would look like we are trying to hush it up or whitewash it."

Under pressure from Democrats, the question quickly shifted from whether there would be an investigation to who would investigate. The Democratic minority on McCarthy's subcommittee wanted the parent Committee on Government Operations to handle the matter, because the larger committee contained an anti-McCarthy majority. However, the Republican members on the Permanent Subcommittee on Investigations voted to have McCarthy's own subcommittee probe the Army's charges against him and his chief counsel.

This unusual step required changes in the subcommittee's makeup. As one of the subjects of the inquiry, McCarthy stepped down from the subcommittee chairmanship. Democrats, with some help from Republicans, also forced McCarthy to remove himself temporarily from the subcommittee itself during the investigation. His seat on the panel was taken by a sympathizer, Senator Henry C. Dworshak of Idaho. Senator Karl Mundt, a South Dakota Republican, reluctantly took over as chairman. Facing reelection that year, Mundt did not relish being on the hot seat; clearly uncomfortable, he had a hard time keeping a tight rein on the proceedings. The other Republicans on the subcommittee were Dirksen of Illinois and Potter of Michigan. In addition to McClellan of Arkansas, the Democratic members were Henry Jackson of Washington and Stuart Symington of Missouri. As chief counsel to replace Roy Cohn for the course of the inquiry, the panel selected Ray H. Jenkins, a Republican lawyer from Tennessee who claimed to have "no record, publicly or otherwise, with regard to Senator McCarthy or what has come to be called McCarthyism."

The subcommittee also had to decide important questions of procedure. Although McCarthy was not a member of the panel, he was given the right to cross-examine witnesses. This insured that the grand inquisitor himself would play an active role in the inquiry. In another unusual step, the subcommittee also granted the Army the privilege of cross-examining witnesses. To handle its case, the Army selected a sixty-three-year-old Boston trial lawyer, Joseph Nye Welch. Puckish-looking, this easygoing gentleman turned out to be the Army's secret weapon. Welch's outward manner concealed a brilliant mind and a biting humor that made him the hit of the proceedings.

Democrats succeeded in getting the dramatic showdown between McCarthy and the Army televised nationally. This gave eighty million Americans a direct look at the proceedings of their government, and the presence of Joe McCarthy guaranteed that the spectators would not be bored. The Army–McCarthy hearings were, above all, a dramatic experience that aroused emotional rather than intellectual responses. Indeed, the legal and political results of the inquiry were inconclusive.

On April 22, 1954, the reconstituted Permanent Subcommittee on Investigations opened its public hearings. The scene in the Senate Caucus Room reflected the attention that the spectacle would receive. The overflow crowd included 500 spectators, 130 reporters and 60 photographers. In addition, there were the TV cameras, lights and recording equipment necessary for the live broadcast, which was carried by all three television networks and by major radio stations. The seven members of the subcommittee sat at the end of the Caucus Room behind a table thirty-five feet long. Chairman Mundt was seated at the center, with Chief Counsel Jenkins and the three Republican members to the left, as viewed by the audience. To the right sat the three Democratic senators, and beyond them at the end of the table were McCarthy and Roy Cohn. Both McCarthy and Cohn had decided against hiring lawyers to assist them; they would do their own cross-examining. Facing the subcommittee was a smaller table for witnesses and the Army's counsel, Joseph Welch. Behind the witness table were seats for spectators, and the first rows were filled with high-ranking army officers in uniform.

At 10:30 A.M. Chairman Mundt pounded his gavel and brought the noisy room to order. He went on to read an opening statement in which he explained how the hearings would proceed. Jenkins would call witnesses and question them first. Then the subcommittee members and Senator McCarthy would take turns cross-examining. Joseph Welch would also get his chance to question witnesses.

No sooner had Mundt explained the rules than McCarthy showed he would not be bound by them. "Mr. Chairman," McCarthy interjected. "A point of order, Mr. Chairman."

"Let the Senator state his point," Mundt responded.

McCarthy proceeded to start a speech complaining that "a few Pentagon politicians, attempting to disrupt our investigations, are naming themselves the Department of the Army."

After listening for a few minutes, Mundt cut off McCarthy, overruled his point of order and warned him against making speeches disguised as a point of order.

McCarthy had failed to win his point of order, but he had won the first battle of words. It was obvious that he would try to dominate the proceedings by interrupting at will and making speeches. The grand inquisitor would become the grand interrupter, with the same old objective of keeping the spotlight of publicity on himself.

In his cross-examination of the first witness, McCarthy resorted to a familiar technique. The lead-off witness was Major General Miles Reber, who described early attempts by McCarthy and Cohn to get an officer's commission for Schine. When McCarthy got his turn to cross-examine, he asked, "Is Sam Reber your brother?" After the general said yes, McCarthy went on to give the false impression that Reber's brother had resigned from the State Department as "a bad security risk." This smear, of course, had nothing to do with the general's testimony. Moreover, there was no way of immediately verifying the accuracy of McCarthy's accusation. However, McCarthy's strategy of implying guilt by association undoubtedly raised questions in the minds of his audience about the witness's testimony, and, more important, the dramatic charge gave McCarthy the attention he eagerly sought.

In part because of McCarthy's disruptive tactics, the hearings became a series of incidents rather than an orderly search for the facts in the dispute between McCarthy and the Army.

Secretary of the Army Robert Stevens presented the Army's case in fourteen long days of testimony. Stevens faced constant interruption from McCarthy, who shouted from his end of the table, "Mr. Chairman, a point of order." Although often cut off in midsentence and overruled by Senator Mundt, McCarthy used these outbursts to grab attention and rattle the witness. Hounded by McCarthy and repeatedly cross-examined by Jenkins, Stevens began to show the strain of the ordeal that had begun the previous July when Schine received his draft notice. Referring to the numerous attempts by McCarthy and Cohn to get special treatment for Schine, Secretary Stevens concluded, "I may say that during my tenure as Secretary of the Army, there is no record that matches this persistent, tireless effort to obtain special consideration and privileges for this man."

In his cross-examination of Stevens, subcommittee counsel Ray Jenkins attempted to show that the Army Secretary might have tried to please McCarthy. As evidence, Jenkins held up a photograph of Stevens and Private Schine. Jenkins suggested that the picture of the two smiling men proved that Stevens was "especially nice and considerate of this boy Schine . . . in order to dissuade the Senator [McCarthy] from continuing his investigation."

Stevens responded that this was completely untrue, but he was clearly surprised by the photo of himself and Schine posing alone like two good friends.

The following day Army Counsel Joseph Welch showed that there was more to the picture than met the eye. Welch charged that the photograph had been "doctored or altered." With the spectators shocked into silence and the television cameras focused on him, Welch continued. "I charge that what was offered in evidence yesterday was an altered, shamefully cut down picture, so that somebody could say to Stevens, 'Were you not photographed alone with David Schine?,' when the truth is he was photographed in a group." Welch then offered "the original, undoctored, unaltered piece of evidence," which showed Stevens, Schine, and a third man, a colonel who commanded the base where the picture was taken.

Upon hearing Welch's description of the original photo, McCarthy exclaimed, "Point of order!" He went on to argue that Welch made "the completely false statement that this is a group picture, and it is not."

Chairman Mundt broke in to say that McCarthy was "engaging in a statement or cross-examination rather than a point of order."

McCarthy responded, "I am getting rather sick of being interrupted in the middle of a sentence."

"If this is not a point of order, it is out of order," Senator Symington advised.

"Oh, be quiet!" barked McCarthy.

Clearly tired of McCarthy's outbursts, Symington replied, "I haven't the slightest intention of being quiet. Counsel is running this committee, and you are not running it."

Disregarding Symington's lecture, McCarthy continued to give his interpretation of the photograph.

After McCarthy finished his diversion, a search began

for the source of the cropped photograph. Joseph Welch made it clear that he did not suspect Ray Jenkins, who had simply introduced the disputed picture. Jenkins testified that he had received the cropped photo from a member of McCarthy's staff. During several days of testimony, witness after witness traced the course of the photo's trip from David Schine's office wall to the hearing room. Schine and Cohn disclaimed any responsibility for altering the original picture. A member of McCarthy's staff, James Juliana, finally admitted that he had arranged for the original photo to be blown up to show just Stevens and Schine. Asked why he had ordered this change, Juliana replied vaguely that he had gotten the idea "Jenkins and/or Cohn" wanted a picture of only Stevens and Schine.

Joseph Welch's questioning of Juliana produced one of the more humorous exchanges that indicated that the Army's counsel was more than a match for McCarthy. Asked by Welch about the source of the original photograph, Juliana said he did not know.

"Did you think this came from a pixie?" Welch inquired.

When this question provoked laughter, McCarthy requested that it be repeated. He then jokingly said to Welch, "Would Counsel, for my benefit, define—I think he might be an expert on this—the word 'pixie'?"

"I should say, Mr. Senator, that a pixie is a close relative of a fairy. Shall I proceed, sir? Have I enlightened you?"

Welch's response sparked another outburst of laughter, but McCarthy just frowned, aware that he, not Welch, had been made to look foolish.

This exchange brought to an end the debate over the cropped photo. Other than its value as entertainment, the incident proved little except that McCarthy's staff would distort evidence in order to make the Army look bad.

120

Another attempt to use phony evidence also blew up in McCarthy's face. On May 4, while cross-examining Stevens, McCarthy whipped out a copy of a letter from the FBI which the Senator said warned the Army that dangerous persons were employed at the Fort Monmouth radar laboratories. Dated January 26, 1951, and supposedly signed by FBI Director J. Edgar Hoover, the letter, according to McCarthy, was still in Army files and should have been acted upon by Secretary Stevens if he had wanted to eliminate threats to American security.

Caught by surprise, Joseph Welch tried to defuse McCarthy's latest bombshell. The army counsel questioned the source of the copy. Addressing Senator McCarthy, Welch declared, "this purported copy did not come from the Army files, and you know I'm quite right, sir, and I have an absorbing curiosity to know how in the dickens you got hold of it."

Disregarding Welch, McCarthy asked Stevens to read the letter. The Army Secretary immediately questioned "whether or not I'm at liberty to discuss a letter from Mr. J. Edgar Hoover." Taking the letter from Stevens, Joseph Welch noted, "It's headed 'Personal and Confidential, Via Liaison,' which seem to be rather severe words of a confidential nature." Welch suggested that the letter ought to be released by J. Edgar Hoover before there was any discussion of it in the hearing room. The committee agreed, and adjourned until the following day.

Robert A. Collier, a subcommittee assistant, contacted Hoover and returned to testify the next day. According to Collier, Hoover stated that he had neither written nor signed any such letter. However, Hoover said, the two-page letter in question did contain some word-for-word statements from a fifteen-page FBI report. Upon hearing this, Joseph Welch triumphantly cross-examined Collier to drive home the point that Senator McCarthy had introduced a fake letter.

"Now, Mr. Collier, as I understand your testimony, this document that I hold in my hand is a carbon copy of precisely nothing," Welch emphasized. "Is that right?"

"I will say that Mr. Hoover informed me that it is not a carbon copy of a memorandum prepared or sent by the FBI," Collier responded.

"Let's have it straight from the shoulder," Welch persisted. "So far as you know, it's a carbon copy of precisely nothing."

"So far as I know, it is. Yes. But that, again, is a —"

"And so far as you know," Welch interrupted, "this document in this courtroom, sprung yesterday by Senator McCarthy, is a perfect phony. Is that right?"

"No sir," Collier answered. "That is your conclusion. I will not uphold such a conclusion."

In an attempt to save face, McCarthy himself took the witness chair. This was one of the rare occasions when the Wisconsin Senator testified under oath. Asked where he had gotten the document in question, McCarthy bravely declared, "I will not under any circumstances reveal the source of any information which I get as chairman of the committee. Now, one of the reasons that I have been successful, I believe, to some extent in exposing Communism is because the people who give me information from within the government know that their confidence will not be violated. There is no way on earth that any committee, any force, can get me to violate the confidence of those people."

Asked by Jenkins whether the document had come from the FBI or from someone in the Army, McCarthy replied that he had gotten it from an Army Intelligence officer.

When McCarthy refused to be more specific, Welch

reminded the Senator that he had taken an oath which "included a promise, a solemn promise by you to tell the truth, comma, the whole truth, comma, and nothing but the truth."

McCarthy responded that he understood the oath.

"And when you took it," Welch teased, "did you have some mental reservations, some Fifth or Sixth Amendment notion that you could measure what you would tell?"

"I don't take the Fifth or Sixth Amendment," McCarthy insisted.

"Then tell us who delivered the document to you," Welch continued.

"Mr. Welch, I think I made it very clear to you that neither you nor anyone else will ever get me to violate the confidence of loyal people in this government who give me information about Communist infiltration. I repeat, you will not get their names, you will not get any information which will allow you to identify them so that you or anyone else can get their jobs. You can go right ahead and try until doomsday."

Senator McClellan then interjected the thought that McCarthy was setting himself above the law by releasing classified information.

"I am not setting myself above the law," McCarthy countered. "But, Senator, I just will not abide by any secrecy directive of anyone."

As this digression continued, Senator Jackson pointed out that "in this now famous two-and-a-quarter-page document, there were about thirty-five names listed. This is pretty serious. Have we had anything this serious so far?"

Using this opening to divert attention further from the phony Hoover letter, McCarthy declared, "I think we've got a much more serious situation now in the Communist infiltration of the CIA." Continuing on this track, McCarthy told his national audience, "I have also discussed with the committee the question of Communist infiltration of atomic- and hydrogen-bomb plants."

McClellan tried in vain to get more information on these latest charges. Meanwhile, the search for the source of the fake letter sputtered to an end.

The Army's case against McCarthy and Cohn focused largely on Cohn. Transcripts of telephone conversations revealed that Roy Cohn had frequently called Defense Department officials, first to seek a commission for Schine and then, failing that, to request special favors, such as getting Private Schine released from kitchen duty at Fort Dix. Struck by the thought that the Secretary of the Army would occupy himself with such questions, Senator McClellan asked the Army's regular counsel, John G. Adams, if it was at all unusual. "It's so unusual, sir, that it's nothing short of fantastic," Adams replied.

Adams also testified that he had often been abused by Cohn, who used obscenities when angry. Although the Army was unable to prove that Cohn had used obscene language, evidence of Cohn's short fuse was plentiful. Secretary Stevens testified that on the occasion when he accompanied McCarthy and his staff on a tour of Fort Monmouth, the group had been confronted with the problem of entering a laboratory where special security clearance was required. Uncertain how to handle the situation, Stevens had decided to permit only elected officials to see the secret laboratory. This barred Roy Cohn and other McCarthy staff members, who waited outside.

"Upon leaving the laboratory," Stevens testified, "I could see that Mr. Cohn was extremely angry at not having been allowed to enter."

124

According to an army officer who had stood waiting with Cohn, McCarthy's chief counsel had exclaimed, "This is war! I am cleared for the highest classified information. I have access to FBI files when I want them. They did this just to embarrass me. We will really investigate the Army now."

Army Counsel John Adams also testified that he had witnessed one of Cohn's temper tantrums. The incident had occurred after Adams accepted Cohn's offer of a ride in New York City. When Adams told Cohn that they were going in the wrong direction, Cohn "in a final fit of violence stopped the car in the middle of four lanes of traffic and said, 'Get there however you can.'" The Army's counsel was left standing in the middle of Park Avenue while Cohn drove away.

In testimony at the Army–McCarthy hearings, Roy Cohn denied he had used obscenities or ever declared war on the Army. However, Cohn's behavior during the hearings reinforced his reputation as a hot-tempered young man who bullied opponents. After one session in which Senator Jackson had sharply cross-examined McCarthy, Cohn approached Robert F. Kennedy, who served as counsel for the subcommittee's Democrats. According to those present, Cohn threatened to go after Jackson by revealing "stuff about his being favorably inclined toward Communists." Reportedly the young Kennedy then challenged Cohn, and the two almost came to blows.

As related by author Fred J. Cook, Cohn told Kennedy, "You have a personal hatred—"

"If I have, it's justified," responded Kennedy.

Cohn flared, "Do you want to fight now?"

Kennedy shot back, "You can't get away with it, Cohn. You tried it with McCarthy and you tried it with the Army. You can't do it."

"Do you think you're qualified to sit here?" Cohn yelled.

At that, Kennedy turned and walked away.

The most dramatic encounter of the hearings came on June 9, 1954, when Joseph Welch cross-examined Roy Cohn. Welch, the experienced trial lawyer, clearly tried to unnerve McCarthy's chief counsel by sarcastically ridiculing charges about Communists in government.

"Mr. Cohn, what is the exact number of Communists or subversives that are loose today in these defense plants?" inquired Welch. When Cohn hesitated, Welch added, "I'm in a hurry. I don't want the sun to go down while they're still in there if we can get them out."

After Cohn indicated there were approximately 130 security risks in sixteen defense plants, Welch suggested, "Will you not, before the sun goes down, give those names to the FBI and at least have those men put under surveillance?"

This comment forced Cohn to admit that the FBI undoubtedly knew about the 130 people.

"Then what's all the excitement about if J. Edgar Hoover is on the job, chasing those 130 Communists?" Welch demanded.

Seeing his chief counsel trapped by Welch's logic, Senator McCarthy rushed to Cohn's rescue. Without even going through the formality of making a point of order, McCarthy blurted out one of his most reckless charges.

"Mr. Chairman," he began, "in view of Mr. Welch's request that the information be given if we know of anyone who might be performing any work for the Communist Party, I think we should tell him that he has in his law firm a young man named Fisher whom he recommended, incidentally, to do the work on this committee, who has been for a number of years a member of an organization which is named, oh, years and years ago, as the legal bulwark of the Communist Party."

Roy Cohn, apparently aware of what his boss was up to, looked at McCarthy in dismay and shook his head as if to say, "Don't do this."

McCarthy, however, persisted. He charged that Frederick G. Fisher, a member of Welch's Boston law firm, had belonged to the National Lawyers' Guild, which had been branded a Communist-front group. Furthermore, McCarthy accused Welch of recommending that Fisher be appointed assistant counsel for the Senate committee investigating the Army–McCarthy dispute.

"I have hesitated bringing that up," McCarthy explained to Welch, "but I have been rather bored with your phony requests to Mr. Cohn here that he personally get every Communist out of government before sundown." McCarthy added that he assumed Welch did not know about Fisher's background.

"I don't think you yourself would ever knowingly aid the Communist cause," McCarthy said to Welch. "I think you're unknowingly siding with it when you try to burlesque this hearing in which we're attempting to bring out the facts."

This smear proved too much for Senator Mundt, a longtime McCarthy supporter, who tried to set the record straight. Mundt observed that he had "no memory of Mr. Welch recommending either Mr. Fisher or anybody else as counsel for this committee."

McCarthy immediately said something about getting a news story to prove his point, but another voice interrupted. It was that of Joseph Welch, who was obviously shocked and angered by what he had just heard. Slowly and deliberately, Welch personally addressed McCarthy in a tone that displayed both sincerity and anguish.

"May I have your attention," Welch began.

McCarthy, however, pretended to be busy ordering his staff to find the evidence on Fred Fisher. "I can listen with one ear," McCarthy said with a laugh.

"Now this time, sir, I want you to listen with both," Welch snapped as he leaned over the microphone. "Senator, you won't need anything in the record when I finish telling you this," he noted, his voice shaking with controlled anger.

"Until this moment, Senator, I think I never really gauged your cruelty or your recklessness," Welch continued. He explained that Fred Fisher, a Harvard Law School graduate and a fellow lawyer in the firm of Hale & Dorr, had been chosen to assist Welch in the Army–McCarthy hearings. When asked by Welch if there was anything in his past that might come out in the hearings and harm the case, Fisher had said, "Mr. Welch, when I was in law school, and for a period of months after, I belonged to the Lawyers' Guild." According to Welch, he had responded, "Fred, I just don't think I'm going to ask you to work on the case. If I do, one of these days that will come out and go over national television, and it will hurt like the dickens."

"And so, Senator, I asked him to go back to Boston," Welch concluded. "Little did I dream you could be so reckless and so cruel as to do an injury to that lad. It is true, he is still with Hale & Dorr. It is true that he will continue to be with Hale & Dorr. It is, I regret to say, equally true that I fear he shall always bear a scar needlessly inflicted by you. If it were in my power to forgive you for your reckless cruelty, I would do so. I like to think I'm a gentle man, but your forgiveness will have to come from someone other than me."

Unwilling to drop the matter, McCarthy started to repeat his charges against Fisher.

128

Welch cut him off, saying, "Let us not assassinate this lad further, Senator. You've done enough. Have you no sense of decency, sir, at long last? Have you left no sense of decency?"

"I know this hurts you, Mr. Welch," McCarthy exclaimed.

"I'll say it hurts," Welch admitted, but he noted, "Senator, I think it hurts you too."

McCarthy still refused to back off, and he persisted in trying to question Welch about Fisher.

Finally Welch declared solemnly, "Mr. McCarthy, I will not discuss this further with you. You have sat within six feet of me and could have asked me about Fred Fisher. You have seen fit to bring it out, and if there is a God in heaven it will do neither you nor your cause any good. I will not discuss it further. I will not ask Mr. Cohn any more questions. You, Mr. Chairman, may, if you will, call the next witness."

The spectators roared their approval of Welch's rebuke with a booming round of applause. Unable to quiet the noise, Chairman Mundt called a recess.

McCarthy stood dumbfounded. After four years of smearing people, he could not understand what he had done wrong.

McCarthy had in fact learned nothing from Welch's lecture. Several days later the Wisconsin Senator baited Stuart Symington, the Missouri Democrat. Challenging Symington to testify under oath about conversations with Army Secretary Stevens, McCarthy referred to his colleague as "sanctimonious Stu."

"I resent that reference to my first name," Symington responded. He also suggested to McCarthy, "You ought to go to a psychiatrist."

"Mr. Symington, . . . I'm glad we're on television," McCarthy said, preparing another zinger. "I think that the millions of people can see how low a man can sink. I repeat, they see how low an *alleged* man can sink."

"Senator, let me tell you something," Symington shot back. "The American people have had a look at you for six weeks. You're not fooling anyone." The Missouri Senator went on to charge that the subcommittee's staff had not exercised sufficient care in guarding files which contained confidential information. He shouted at McCarthy, "I think the files of what you call 'my staff,' 'my director,' 'my chief of staff,' have been the sloppiest and most dangerously handled files that I have ever known of since I've been in the government."

This rebuke was greeted with applause and the chairman's call for a recess.

As people stood to leave the Caucus Room, McCarthy tried to get in the last words. Accusing Symington of running away and refusing to back up his charge against the committee staff, McCarthy concluded, "May I say that that is the most dishonest, the most unfounded smear upon some of the most outstanding young men that I have ever seen work to uncover Communists."

During the hearings, McCarthy did not confine his attacks to Democrats or representatives of the Army. He also lashed out once again at the Eisenhower administration. Although the President still tried to avoid any confrontation, he found it difficult to escape McCarthy's wrath. The issue that provoked the Senator was Eisenhower's order directing employees of the executive branch not to testify about private discussions that had taken place within the administration. The presidential order resulted from the efforts of the Army–McCarthy inquiry to learn the details of a conference between Army Counsel John G. Adams and other members of the administration. Eisenhower argued that his order was necessary to preserve the separation of powers between the executive branch and Congress.

All the senators on the investigating committee objected to Eisenhower's "gag" order, but McCarthy violently denounced the administration. Calling the order an "iron curtain," McCarthy told reporters it might force Republicans to "commit suicide before the television cameras." Suggesting that the administration "must have something to hide," McCarthy charged in the hearings that the blackout order was "a type of Fifth Amendment privilege." The Wisconsin Senator also publicly encouraged government workers to disobey the President. On May 27 he announced at the hearings, "I would like to notify those two million federal employees that I feel it is their duty to give us any information which they have about graft, corruption, Communism, treason." McCarthy added, "There is no loyalty to a superior officer which can tower above and beyond their loyalty to their country."

Still refusing to "get into the gutter with that guy," Eisenhower did not respond to McCarthy's direct challenge to presidential authority. However, Attorney General Herbert Brownell pointed out that it was the President's duty to enforce the laws, and that "that responsibility can't be usurped by an individual who may seek to set himself above the laws of our land."

Joe McCarthy's performance during the Army–McCarthy hearings deeply troubled Republicans. As the nationally televised hearings dragged on, leading Republicans privately expressed anguish. The Republican national chairman remarked that McCarthy had done the party "more harm than good." The head of the Republican national finance committee called the hearings "a disgraceful affair." Even the Investigations Subcommittee's chairman, Karl Mundt, admitted to a friend "that these hearings are doing neither the country nor the Republican Party any good."

Clearly distressed, Republicans on the subcommittee

repeatedly tried to limit the Army–McCarthy hearings. In May, Senator Dirksen suggested moving the hearings behind closed doors. Republicans also attempted to end the public hearings during a May recess. However, pressure from Democrats and a few words from the President forced the spectacle to continue.

Finally, on June 17, 1954, the hearings came to an end, two and a half months after they had begun. The subcommittee had run out of steam, not out of witnesses. (Private Schine, for example, was never questioned about his treatment.) The Democrats wanted to continue, but Republicans outvoted them to call a halt.

The results of the hearings were inconclusive. Despite all the dramatic incidents, the investigation often strayed from the central issues in the dispute between McCarthy and the Army. Some testimony only clouded the issues rather than clarifying them. Although Joseph Welch sometimes referred to the setting as a "courtroom," the proceedings were a congressional inquiry with no final verdict. Nevertheless, it was clear from the testimony that Senator McCarthy and Roy Cohn had sought special treatment for G. David Schine. McCarthy never produced any evidence that the Army had held Schine as a "hostage" to stop the Senator's probe of the military, but it appeared that Army Secretary Stevens had tried in various ways to sidetrack McCarthy.

On August 31, 1954, the subcommittee finally issued its report on the Army–McCarthy dispute. After two and a half months of sorting through the record, the seven members divided sharply in their conclusions. The Republicans' majority report tried to get McCarthy off the hook by putting most of the blame on Roy Cohn for his "unduly aggressive and persistent" efforts on behalf of his pal, Schine. The Republicans dismissed McCarthy's charge of "blackmail" by the Army, but they criticized Army Secretary Stevens for his "appeasement and vacillation" in the Schine matter. In a minority report, the committee's Democrats also rapped the Army's handling of Schine, but they came down hardest on Senator McCarthy for having condoned Cohn's behavior in the first place and for defending it throughout the hearings. "For these inexcusable actions Senator McCarthy and Mr. Cohn merit severe criticism," the Democrats concluded. Senator Charles Potter, the Michigan Republican, filed his own evenhanded view that "the principal accusation of each side . . . was borne out."

The impact of the Army–McCarthy hearings went far beyond the issues dealt with in the subcommittee's final report. Above all, the televised hearings exposed Joe McCarthy at his worst—disrupting the proceedings, bullying witnesses, insulting fellow senators, advocating insubordination, introducing fake evidence, and smearing persons in no way related to the controversy. These tactics revealed to a national audience the meaning of McCarthyism. One result was a sharp decline in the Senator's popularity. In a Gallup poll, McCarthy's support dropped from its January 1954 peak of 50 percent favorable to him, to only 34 percent favorable in June of the same year. During the same period, the number opposed to him rose from 29 percent to 45 percent. By August 1954, a majority of those questioned held an unfavorable view of McCarthy.

In the wake of the Army–McCarthy hearings, some senators chipped away at McCarthy's powers as a committee chairman. Senator Potter joined Democrats on the Investigations Subcommittee who demanded changes in what McCarthy referred to as "my staff." In July, Roy Cohn announced his resignation, which McCarthy "reluctantly" accepted. Additional transfers and reassignments followed. McCarthy then failed to get his choice selected as Cohn's replacement.

Despite these behind-the-scenes maneuvers, most senators still hesitated to challenge McCarthy directly and openly. However, an unusual move by a single senator finally forced the unwilling Senate to confront the issue of Joe McCarthy.

11 | Censure

The blow that doomed Joe McCarthy came from an unexpected quarter. On June 11, 1954, Senator Ralph E. Flanders, a Vermont Republican, entered the Senate Caucus Room as the Army–McCarthy hearings were winding to an end. The seventy-three-year-old Flanders made his way through the crowded hearing room to the witness table, where Senator McCarthy was testifying. With a national television audience looking on, Flanders silently handed McCarthy an envelope. McCarthy read the contents aloud.

"This is to inform you," Flanders had written, "that I plan to make another speech concerning your activities in the Senate this afternoon." The brief note went on to invite McCarthy to attend.

As Flanders turned to leave the Caucus Room, McCarthy dismissed the invitation, saying he would be busy testifying. Besides, he added, "I don't have enough interest in any Flanders speech to listen to it." McCarthy later told reporters, "I think they should get a net and take him to a good quiet place."

Flanders, however, forced McCarthy, the full Senate and the entire nation to sit up and take notice. The mention of "another" speech in Flanders' note referred to the fact that the Senator had begun speaking out against McCarthy several months earlier. He had given his first anti-McCarthy speech in March, just two days before the Army released its "chronology" of the Schine affair. In another address on June 1, he had compared McCarthy to Hitler and accused him of dividing the country. "Were the junior Senator from Wisconsin in the pay of the Communists he could not have done a better job for them," Flanders had concluded.

Senator Flanders seemed an unlikely candidate to lead the charge against McCarthy. Born into a Vermont family of poor farmers, Flanders had gone from rags to riches and was fundamentally a conservative who thought "the New Deal was possessed of ideas which closely paralleled the Communists." Flanders was also a deeply spiritual man.

His strong moral sense was apparently offended by the extremes of McCarthyism. He had privately expressed his reservations about the Wisconsin Senator, and he had even drawn up an anti-McCarthy resolution in 1951. However, Flanders had hesitated to come out openly against McCarthy. He hoped someone else, such as Eisenhower or the Democrats, would curb McCarthy. "I shall have to leave to the Democrats the problem of making a case for the expulsion of a Republican Senator," he wrote in 1953. "I hope you will not think that I am cynical on this matter because I am disturbed by the situation, but I have to decide what is the wisest use of my time."

When this mild-mannered Republican finally spoke out

against McCarthy in 1954, he initially failed to rouse his colleagues to action, so he forced the issue. On June 11 he introduced a Senate resolution which formally condemned McCarthy's conduct and called for his removal as a committee chairman if he did not answer certain questions about his past behavior in the Senate. According to Senate rules, a resolution is assigned to a committee and then voted on by the full Senate if approved by committee members. Thus it was possible for senators to bury Flanders' resolution if they still wished to avoid the issue of McCarthy.

The initial reaction to Flanders' surprise move was consternation among leading Republicans and Democrats. Republican Majority Leader William F. Knowland immediately declared, "I don't believe the motion entered was justified." A member of Eisenhower's Cabinet asked Flanders to "lay off." For different reasons, many Democrats showed little enthusiasm for Flanders' resolution. Still viewing McCarthy as the responsibility of Republicans, one Democrat observed, "Joe's their problem, let them battle it out." Some Democrats, especially Southerners, were troubled about the idea of dumping a committee chairman through a Senate resolution. "If we get back in power we don't want a simple motion like Senator Flanders' to throw us out of joint," one Democrat remarked. Many senators also did not relish the thought of voting on McCarthy during an election year.

This kind of sentiment made the prospects for Flanders' resolution look dim. "The greatest stumbling block," wrote one observer, "is the alliance between the Republican and Democratic leadership . . . which is trying [to] mousetrap the Flanders motion."

Nevertheless, the Senator from Vermont refused to back off. "I agree this is embarrassing to the Republican leader-

137

ship," Flanders commented, "but it's past time for them to be talking about that now." A few Democratic senators supported Flanders' effort. Herbert H. Lehman of New York introduced a similar resolution, and Senators Hubert H. Humphrey, A. S. "Mike" Monroney and J. William Fulbright also reportedly agreed to help.

The course of the Flanders resolution was rocky at best. On June 15, four days after its introduction, the resolution was sent to the Senate Rules Committee. Flanders made it clear that he would not let the issue die, but one man, or even a handful of men, could not bring down McCarthy.

Unable to budge many senators, Flanders tried a new tack. On July 16 he announced that he would introduce a new resolution calling for McCarthy's censure, but not for his removal as a committee chairman. While this would clearly lay to rest some objections, it would also, according to Flanders, "permit a clear-cut vote on McCarthyism." The Vermont Senator pointed out that even a vote to amend or table the new resolution would show where senators stood on the issue of McCarthy. "Even absence has significance," he emphasized in an obvious warning to anyone who might try to duck the vote.

The new resolution immediately picked up additional support among Democrats. Southerners in particular showed a greater willingness to back a motion to condemn that did not affect cherished chairmanships. Senators John McClellan and Walter F. George both agreed to vote for a censure motion. However, the Democratic leadership refused to make this a party issue. The Democratic Policy Committee called it "a matter of conscience upon which each individual Senator should vote his convictions without regard to party affiliations."

On July 30, Flanders formally introduced Senate Resolution 301, which asked for the censure of Joseph McCarthy. Three days of heated debate followed. Senator Everett Dirksen sprang to McCarthy's defense by attacking Flanders for being on the same side as the Communists opposed to McCarthy. More to the point, Guy Cordon of Oregon raised procedural questions. He emphasized that Flanders' resolution did not specify what McCarthy had done to deserve censure. Cordon also wanted the resolution to be considered by a committee. Flanders and his allies resisted these changes because they feared, in the words of Senator J. William Fulbright of Arkansas, "Joe can buffalo any committee on earth." Several senators began to list specific charges against McCarthy until they reached a total of forty-six.

On the third day of debate, Majority Leader Knowland finally moved that Flanders' censure resolution and all the suggested amendments be sent to a six-man select committee. The motion passed, 75 to 12, with an amendment calling for a final committee report before that session of Congress adjourned. The twelve negative votes were cast by Flanders and his supporters, who wanted an immediate vote on McCarthy. According to Herbert Lehman, the pro-censure forces had been "temporarily defeated." However, the Senate had only postponed action. The issue of McCarthy's behavior was still very much alive.

Nevertheless, the anti-McCarthy senators had reason to be pessimistic. By 1954 Joe McCarthy had already been the subject of five Senate investigations. In each case the Wisconsin Senator had escaped any formal rebuke. Indeed, he was a master at subverting probes of his activities.

McCarthy's future now depended on another committee of senators. This group, however, was made up of an equal number of Republicans and Democrats, and its sole responsibility was to investigate McCarthy and report its

139

findings before the end of the session, less than six months away. The members of the select committee, chosen by party leaders, were all conservatives who had not previously spoken out on McCarthyism. The three Republicans were Frank Carlson of Kansas, Francis H. Case of South Dakota, and Arthur V. Watkins of Utah, who was named chairman. The Democratic members were Edwin C. Johnson of Colorado, John C. Stennis of Mississippi, and Sam J. Ervin of North Carolina. Although all six qualified as conservatives, the members of the Watkins Committee were widely respected by their Senate colleagues. Indeed, both McCarthy and Flanders expressed satisfaction with the makeup of the select committee, but for different reasons. McCarthy undoubtedly was reassured by their conservatism, while Flanders thought they would restrain McCarthy's disruptive antics. "They will hold the reins," Flanders observed, "and to have someone else hold the reins will be a new experience for the junior Senator from Wisconsin."

The Watkins Committee did in fact take steps to keep McCarthy in check during the course of the investigation. "We are not unmindful of *his* genius for disruption," Watkins reportedly said. During August 1954 the panel developed a set of ground rules that ignored demands made by McCarthy. The committee decided to handle the inquiry somewhat like a court trial. McCarthy was considered "sort of a defendant because charges have been leveled against him," Watkins remarked. The committee denied McCarthy's request that he be given an opportunity to cross-examine his accusers. The panel would collect documentary evidence and testimony only from witnesses with direct knowledge of events. This excluded Flanders and other leading anti-McCarthyites. Furthermore, either McCarthy or his lawyer could cross-examine a witness,

140

but not both. The rules of the select committee not only reduced the possibility of any dramatic confrontation, but also removed the proceedings from the glare of television. The hearings were open to the public, but not televised.

Before any public hearings, the Watkins Committee also reduced the long list of charges to five categories that might be grounds for censure. These specific charges against McCarthy included action in contempt of the Senate, encouragement of federal employees to violate the law, receipt of classified material, and the abuse of Senate colleagues and General Zwicker. All these charges were narrowly conceived and related largely to the breaking of Senate rules or unwritten codes of conduct. Most important, the investigating senators carefully avoided the question of Communism in McCarthy's reckless attacks.

With McCarthy severely straightjacketed and the charges against him specified, the Watkins Committee held its first public hearing on August 31. The setting was the same Senate Caucus Room where the Army–McCarthy hearings had been held, but the scene was vastly different. Gone were the television and newsreel cameras. Gone, too, was the atmosphere of excitement. Apparently aware that his political career was on the line, McCarthy for the first time was accompanied by an attorney, Edward Bennett Williams, one of Washington's best-known and most capable lawyers. Chairman Watkins attested to the significance of the inquiry in his opening statement. "We realize that the United States Senate, in a sense, is on trial," he intoned.

Watkins also showed on the first day that he would keep McCarthy on a tight rein. Toward the end of the first session, McCarthy tried a typical diversion by accusing Senator Johnson of bias for allegedly saying that he loathed the Wisconsin Senator. Cutting McCarthy off,

Chairman Watkins ruled him out of order. McCarthy persisted, but so, too, did Watkins, who repeatedly pounded his gavel. "We are not going to be interrupted by these diversions and sidelines," Watkins exclaimed. The chairman abruptly ended the shouting match by calling a recess. In disbelief, McCarthy called this "the most unheard-of thing I ever heard of."

Anyone expecting additional fireworks was disappointed. The Watkins Committee held only nine public sessions, and most of them were devoted to long recitals of documentary evidence. One newspaperman observed that the committee might not censure McCarthy, "but it may well bore him to death." The difference between the Army–McCarthy hearings and the Watkins investigation, according to another reporter, was like the difference between a Hollywood premiere and a coroner's inquest.

After hearing the evidence, the Watkins Committee listened to rebuttal by McCarthy and his lawyer. However, the pair were frequently cut short by rulings that their presentation was irrelevant. On one occasion, McCarthy even had his comments stricken from the record.

After reviewing the accumulated evidence behind closed doors, the Watkins Committee issued its final report on September 27. The six conservative senators unanimously recommended McCarthy's censure on two charges. One was for contempt of the Senate because he had refused in 1952 to appear before the Subcommittee on Privileges and Elections, which was investigating charges against McCarthy made by Senator Benton. "It was the duty of Senator McCarthy to accept the repeated invitations by the subcommittee," the report stated. "[N]o formal order or subpoena should be necessary to bring Senators before Senate committees when their own honor and the honor of the Senate are at issue." In addition, the Watkins Committee recommended that McCarthy be censured for his "reprehensible" treatment of General Zwicker at the February 1954 hearing during McCarthy's search for the officers responsible for the honorable discharge of Major Peress.

What, then, was Joe McCarthy finally accused of? According to the select committee, the Wisconsin Senator had violated the unwritten rules of the Senate. He had failed to show proper "honor" and had neglected his "duty." This, of course, was scarcely the worst of McCarthy's faults. However, conservative senators were unwilling to come to grips with the issue of McCarthyism and its many victims. After all, the Senate itself had participated in the witch-hunt, and no senator questioned the essential righteousness of the anti-Communist crusade. Instead, the Watkins Committee focused on McCarthy's behavior, which it found ungentlemanly.

The debate in the Senate itself over whether to censure Joe McCarthy made it clear that his colleagues questioned his tactics, not his hostility to Communists. McCarthy added to his problems by viciously attacking Senator Watkins and the select committee. He claimed that three committee members had engaged in "fraud" when they failed to disqualify themselves from the panel. He also referred to the pending Senate debate as a "lynch party." Once the debate got under way on November 10, 1954, McCarthy issued a statement charging the Watkins Committee with having "imitated Communist methods" and having made itself the "involuntary agent" of the Communist conspiracy. McCarthy also called Senator Watkins "cowardly" and "stupid."

These remarks helped seal McCarthy's fate. During the Senate debate, several conservative Democrats denounced the "slush and slime" and the "fantastic and foul accusations" that McCarthy spewed. More important, several

Republicans spoke out strongly in favor of censure. Senator Watkins forcefully put the issue to his colleagues. "Continuous guerrilla warfare has been waged against us by the junior Senator from Wisconsin and his journalistic friends . . . in an effort to put us in bad with the people of the country. It was abuse heaped upon abuse," Watkins argued. "What are you going to do about it?" he challenged his colleagues.

Not a single Democrat defended McCarthy, but a number of Republican "bitter-enders" went to his rescue. Senators Everett Dirksen and Barry Goldwater spoke up for McCarthy. They pictured the censure resolution as part of a Communist plot. "I suggest to the Senate at this time," Goldwater declared, "that if this censure movement against the Senator is successful the next attack will undoubtedly be made upon J. Edgar Hoover." McCarthy's supporters tried unsuccessfully to water down the censure motion.

Outnumbered by his opponents, McCarthy sought delay. On November 17 he entered the hospital for treatment of a swollen elbow. In his absence the Senate adjourned for ten days. However, McCarthy's days were clearly numbered.

When the Senate reconvened on November 29, it voted, against McCarthy's wishes, to limit debate. In the last hours, Senate leaders broke their long silence. Republican Majority Leader William Knowland came out against censure. Minority Leader Lyndon Johnson took a stand against McCarthy. "In my mind, there is only one issue here—morality and conduct," Johnson declared. He claimed that McCarthy's statements about fellow Senators did not belong in *The Congressional Record*, but should be "more fittingly inscribed on the wall of a men's room."

144

After more than four years of riding high, Joe McCarthy met his day of reckoning on December 2, 1954. The Senate voted 67 to 22 to "condemn" McCarthy for his contempt of the Subcommittee on Privileges and Elections and for his abuse of the Watkins Committee and its members. Every Democrat present voted to condemn him, and the Republicans split evenly, 22 for condemnation and 22 against. Three senators did not vote. Alexander Wiley, McCarthy's fellow Republican from Wisconsin, went on a trip to South America, apparently to avoid the issue. John F. Kennedy, the Massachusetts Democrat, was in a New York hospital, and he never revealed how he would have voted. Senator McCarthy simply voted "present" when his named was called.

Slow to move against McCarthy, the Senate clearly had not taken this step lightly. Indeed, rarely in U.S. history had a senator been censured or condemned (the words were often used interchangeably). The last time this had occurred was in 1929.

Nevertheless, Senator McCarthy tried to laugh off the result. When a question arose whether he had been "censured" or "condemned" (the final resolution said "condemned"), McCarthy remarked, "Well, it wasn't exactly a vote of confidence." Asked about his plans, McCarthy exclaimed, "I'm happy to have this circus ended so I can get back to the real work of digging out Communism, crime and corruption."

In fact, the resolution to condemn McCarthy did not take away his committee assignments or any of his Senate privileges. However, time and his own recklessness finally caught up with Joe. Disgraced by the vote of condemnation, he appeared to go over the edge.

Five days after being condemned by the Senate, McCarthy burst into a session of his subcommittee and demanded to make a statement. Angered by President Eisenhower's recent praise of Senator Watkins, he shouted, "They're shooting at me from the other end of the Avenue. I've got to say something." McCarthy went on to argue that he had been "mistaken" to believe that Eisenhower would wage "a vigorous, forceful drive against Communists in government." As a result, he "apologized" to the American people for having asked them to vote for Ike in 1952.

This outburst lost McCarthy most of his remaining allies in the Senate. The attack on Eisenhower drew criticism from most of the Republicans, including Knowland and Goldwater, who had defended McCarthy during the censure debate. The White House confirmed McCarthy's exile by announcing that neither the Senator's name nor his wife's would appear on any future guest list of the Executive Mansion.

McCarthy also lost his committee chairmanship, as a result of the Democrats' victory in the 1954 election. The Senator continued to make speeches and to issue press releases, but no one paid any attention to him. More important, no one was afraid of him anymore. This must have been the greatest blow to McCarthy. He had lost his ability to generate headlines or fear. He was like an aging dog turned loose in the wilderness where no one could hear his bark—which had always been worse than his bite.

The last two and a half years of Joe McCarthy's life were spent in obscurity. Although still a U.S. senator, he was in disgrace. He did not even attend the Republican national convention in 1956, and he stayed out of the campaign. Friends thought he drank more heavily than before, and his body appeared to show the ravaging effects of alcohol. On May 2, 1957, McCarthy died of a liver ailment, at the age of forty-eight.

Conclusion

Joe McCarthy was a product of his times. Like his rise, McCarthy's fall was a result, at least in part, of forces beyond his control. The course of the Cold War was one of these factors. Just as he rose to power with the outbreak of the Korean War in 1950, he fell after an agreement brought an end to the fighting in 1953. The relaxation of Cold War tensions was marked in 1955 by President Eisenhower's first summit conference with Soviet leaders. The Cold War had not ended, but American fears of Communism had noticeably declined.

Joe McCarthy was, of course, neither the first nor the last politician to appeal to an exaggerated fear of Communism. Although his name will forever be identified with reckless and unfounded attacks on innocent persons, he did not invent the practice. Indeed, most victims of so-called McCarthyism suffered at the hands of government officials other than Senator McCarthy. Hundreds of loyal

Americans were fired, blacklisted, discredited and even jailed because of persecution by local, state and federal officials who, like McCarthy, equated dissent with disloyalty. McCarthy's outrageous behavior and his willingness to lie simply made him the most publicized anti-Communist.

When the U.S. Senate finally condemned McCarthy's excesses in 1954, it did not question McCarthyism as such. Senators showed that they could tolerate McCarthy's abusive treatment of left-wingers and liberals who held no elective office, but ultimately they could not forgive his personal attacks on his colleagues in Congress. As Senator Herbert Lehman pointed out after the censure vote, "We have condemned the individual, but we have not yet repudiated the 'ism.'"

As if to prove its continued belief in the anti-Communist cause, the Senate had unanimously passed the Communist Control Act in August 1954. This measure was designed to outlaw the Communist Party. It also required so-called "Communist-infiltrated organizations" to register with the government. By using such a vague term, the law appeared to go a long way toward enacting the kind of guilt by association popularized by McCarthy. However, a liberal Democrat, Senator Hubert Humphrey, defended the bill with the declaration "I am tired of reading headlines about being 'soft' on Communism." According to another liberal senator, Wayne Morse of Oregon, "In the Senate there is no division of opinion among liberals, conservatives and those in between when it comes to our utter detestation of the Communist conspiracy and our united insistence that as a Senate we will fight the growth of the Communist conspiracy."

Through such legislation the practice of McCarthyism outlived McCarthy himself. Guilt by association continued

148

to cost civil servants their jobs under the loyalty-security program set up by President Truman and strengthened by President Eisenhower.

However, Americans gradually recovered from the hysteria that had gripped the country since the end of World War II. Although elected politicians were slow to come to their senses, the Supreme Court finally took the lead in attacking the constitutionality of the government's loyalty-security program. Beginning in 1957, the country's highest court started chipping away at the government's worst practices which had violated civil liberties protected by the Constitution. For example, the Court ruled that someone accused of disloyalty had the right to see the government's files pertaining to him. The Court also curbed the abuses of congressional committees and freed several Communists from jail. In the 1960s, the Court finally threw out sections of the Subversive Activities Control Act of 1950 and the Communist Control Act of 1954.

These decisions reflected the legal opinion that the executive and legislative branches of the federal government had trampled on individual rights during the panic created by the Cold War. Joe McCarthy was not the only offender, but he was the best-known practitioner of what will always be remembered as McCarthyism.

Selected Bibliography

Anderson, Jack, and Ronald W. May. *McCarthy: The Man, the Senator, the "Ism."* Boston, 1952.

Buckley, William F., Jr., and L. Brent Bozell. *McCarthy and His Enemies: The Record and Its Meaning.* Chicago, 1954.

Caute, David. *The Great Fear: The Anti-Communist Purge under Truman and Eisenhower.* New York, 1978.

Cook, Fred J. *The Nightmare Decade: The Life and Times of Senator Joe McCarthy.* New York, 1971.

Crosby, Donald. *God, Church, and Flag: Senator Joseph R. McCarthy and the Catholic Church, 1950–1957.* Chapel Hill, N.C., 1978.

Freeland, Richard M. *The Truman Doctrine and the Origins of McCarthyism: Foreign Policy, Domestic Politics, and Internal Security, 1946–1948.* New York, 1972.

Griffith, Robert. *The Politics of Fear: Joseph R. McCarthy and the Senate.* Lexington, Ky., 1970.

Griffith, Robert, and Athan Theoharis, eds., *The Spectre: Original Essays on the Cold War and the Origins of McCarthyism*. New York, 1974.

Harper, Alan D. *The Politics of Loyalty: The White House and the Communist Issue, 1946–1952*. Westport, Conn., 1969.

Latham, Earl. *The Communist Controversy in Washington from the New Deal to McCarthy*. Cambridge, Mass., 1966.

O'Brien, Michael. *McCarthy and McCarthyism in Wisconsin*. Columbia, Mo., 1980.

Reeves, Thomas C. "The Search for Joe McCarthy," *Wisconsin Magazine of History*, 60 (Spring 1977), 185–96.

————. "Tail Gunner Joe: Joseph R. McCarthy and the Marine Corps," *Wisconsin Magazine of History*, 62 (Summer 1979), 300–313.

Rogin, Michael P. *McCarthy and the Intellectuals: The Radical Specter*. Cambridge, Mass., 1967.

Rovere, Richard H. *Senator Joe McCarthy*. Cleveland, 1959.

Theoharis, Athan. *Seeds of Repression: Harry S. Truman and the Origins of McCarthyism*. Chicago, 1971.

Thomas, Lately. *When Even Angels Wept: The Senator Joseph McCarthy Affair—A Story without a Hero*. New York, 1973.

Index

About the Author

Robert P. Ingalls received an undergraduate degree from Purdue University in Indiana and a master's degree and doctorate in history from Columbia University in New York City.

He has written a number of articles for academic journals and published two books: HERBERT H. LEHMAN AND NEW YORK'S LITTLE NEW DEAL with New York University Press, and HOODS: THE STORY OF THE KU KLUX KLAN with Putnam's. His work was also anthologized in a collection edited by C. Vann Woodward. In 1974 he served as Consultant to the Impeachment Inquiry Staff of the House Committee on the Judiciary.

Mr. Ingalls is currently an Associate Professor of History and Department Chairman at the University of South Florida in Tampa, where he lives with his wife, Joèle, and their two children, Michèle and Marc.